A 15 minute "Date" with God

STRENGTHEN YOUR RELATIONSHIP IN 3 WAYS

CANDICE REYES

ISBN- 978-0-578-67650-0

Join our Scripture of the Day Devotions by subscribing to our website www.Hooks2Crook.com. You can also join our Facebook Group https://www.facebook.com/groups/hooks2crooksod, https://www.instagram.com/hooks2crook, or Twitter@Hooks2C

Book Cover Photo by Jose Hurtado III, 2020

Acknowledgment:

First, I want to thank God: Heavenly Father, YOU are my sustainer. You are my portion, and I am entirely devoted to you. Thank you, Lord, for your armor that protects me every single day. I cherish our dates in the mornings, for your abundant love pours out and covers me from the top of my head to the tips of my toes. You never stop amazing me. Father, it is because of my love and adoration for you that grew from our dates I share this formation publicly. I hope to inspire and encourage others to schedule "Dates" of their own with you every morning. May those first 15 minutes of their day with you be honey to their lips, the air in their lungs, and peace in their soul.

Second, I want to thank ALL the Women Bible Study ROCKSTARS: Ladies, thank you for publishing Bible Studies and videos with lessons so rich in God's Word. It's through your inspirational teachings I was encouraged to learn and grow in my relationship with God. It is because of your passion for the Lord I was inspired to dig deeper with my studies. Your love for Jesus was the seed I needed to bear this fruit. Thank you for leading other ladies in their faith through your relationship with God.

Third, members of my committee and editing team: I am grateful for the lessons and training I received through *Hope Writers*. The skills and resources *Hope Writers* provided encouraged and equipped me to step out of my comfort zone. Thank you to the men and women who helped advise and support my journey. It is because of your love for the Lord and your dear friendship this book exists. Thank you to my editorial *Elisa A. Garza* for editing and proofreading my work before publishing.

Last, but not even close to be the least, I want to thank my family: My heart is overwhelmed by the support and encouragement my family has offered. Thank you for being a safe place for me to lean on when trials knock at my door. God blessed me when He wove me into your stories. As I watch you walk out your faith, I have learned so much. I am so thankful to have each of you in my life. Thank you for always having my back and cheering me onto victory in Jesus.

About the Author:

Candice Reyes: writes regularly on her blog, Hooks2Crook, and a Scripture of the Day Devotion once or twice a week for her subscribers. She is a speaker, teacher, and writer, with a message of encouragement, Biblical equipping principles, and endorses other women to be obedient to the Lord as they use their gifts for His glory. Candice has an amazing husband, Elias, who is her BIGGEST cheerleader—partnering together as they raise their three amazing children. Ministry has a special place in her heart, but her priority is to be a loving wife and a present mother. Candice lives in the great city of Katy, TX.

Table of Contents:

Introduction:

We all have a longing in our souls that remains unfilled. No matter how many books we read, the foods we eat, the classes we take, or how successful we become, it all leads to discontentment. Would you agree? The feeling that there must be more to life than this has plagued my mind for too long. Can you relate?

I found a way to quiet that voice that is never satisfied by replacing it with the voice of God.

When the Lord knit us in our mothers' wombs, He created a space inside us that only He could fill. However, we keep trying to place a square peg in a round hole, thinking one day it will fit. Guess what? The square peg will never match the round hole.

We are designed to long for an intimate relationship with God.

God desires time with you. He is the only one who can fill the void you so desperately try to suppress. Over the years, I attempted to fill that vacancy with other things as I strived towards "success." Every endeavor, I would fill my hole with empty promises and chocolate. Each failed attempt, my loneliness grew, and so did my pant size until I changed my approach.

Would you like to know how I did this?

I schedule "dates" with the Lord every morning. Yep, every MORNING. Before you tune me out, let me explain. Earlier on in my life, I would have skipped right past that word. I love my sleep, too.

It is in the mornings I gather the nourishment God provides to last me for the day. *Lysa TerKeurst* calls God's Word *"manna"*[4]. And I believe she is onto something with that reference. I believe manna comes from the complete practice of Prayer, Reading Scripture, and Praise and is fresh in the mornings.

> *Then the Lord said to Moses, "I am going to rain bread from heaven for you. The people are to go out each day and gather enough for that day. This way I will test them to see whether or not they will follow My instructions. On the sixth day, when they prepare what they bring in, it will be twice as much as they gather on other days."*
>
> *-Exodus 16:4-5 (HCSB)*

The manna I receive from my 15 minute "dates" with God are tucked into my heart for that day. Each morning He replenishes my weary body with grace and joy filling my gaping hole with Jesus. Every crevice in my heart is filled and sealed. Following the example Jesus set, I rise with anticipation as I get ready for my "date" with the Lord.

> *"Very early in the morning, while it was still dark, Jesus got up, left the house and went off to a solitary place, where he prayed."*
>
> *-Mark 1:35 (NIV)*

Captivated by the Lover of my soul I rise early in the morning.

When starting this new routine, I noticed on mornings I skipped my "date" with the Lord I would end up striving in my own strength throughout the whole day. Exhaustion would hit me like a ton of bricks. My head ended up on my pillow, never spending time at the feet of Jesus. And when a storm hit, my feet would be knocked out from underneath me unable to stand firm against the raging winds.

As I keep my dates with the LORD, and I follow the example of Jesus, the less I strive in my own strength, and the more I rely on Him to get me through the day.

Before you put this book back on the self, because mornings are already hard enough and to add something else just doesn't sound appealing, I have a question:

Could you spare 15 minutes in your day? Would you be willing to pencil God's name over those 15 minutes on your schedule? Can you place those 15 minutes at the beginning of your day?

Maybe you already meet with the Lord daily. This study will offer ways to fine-tune your "dates." Please hear me out. My daughter plays volleyball with the hope of playing for college. This year, to save money, we chose to hold off on private lessons because she plays so often. Since she was knowledgeable about technique, we felt a private lesson would be a waste of money.

Until one game during her warm-up, my husband noticed our daughter's form and stance were lax, causing some minor errors. The following week, a couple of the girls on her team scheduled a group lesson to prep for the next tournament and invited our daughter to join them. We agreed the session would be good for her.

When my husband and daughter returned from the lesson, irritation was written all over her face. I inquired about the look. My husband explained the private session covered **FUNDAMENTALS!**

Our daughter received a training on the skills she needed to maintain to strengthen her performance. Foundational techniques and body posture affect her game, proving the lesson was beneficial.

Sometimes a refresher might not sound appealing and learning something new isn't what we need. However, with the right perspective, *growth can flourish from God's simple reminders*. This book, for some, might be just the refresher to help you with your stride.

This book, if given a chance, might amaze you how 15 minutes with God can fill the hole that lingers inside. These are the steps I use in my own 15 minute "Date" with God.

> *"While they stood in their places, they read from the book of the law of the LORD their God for a fourth of the day and spent another fourth of the day in confession and worship of the LORD their God."*
>
> *-Nehemiah 9:3 (HCSB)*

My morning "Dates" consist of three different activities: Prayer, Reading Scripture, and Praising God lasting about an hour long. As I continued to meet with God in the mornings, I learned more about Him, and that knowledge increased my faith and love for Him. I desperately wanted others to know Him this way but knew an hour would turn most of them away. So, I began praying seeking wisdom from God on how could this become more enticing for others to try?

God answered my prayer while attending my son's church. At the end of the service, his pastor mentioned a simple break down of the process but in a manageable 15 Minutes. Pastor Jeremy used my same break down but suggested each section to only last five minutes. His suggestion of 15 Minutes a day was the answer I was seeking. Even the busiest person could find time to meet with the Lord for 15 Minutes a day.

God knows His plans for our day. Morning "dates" help me check in with the driver before I get into the car. As I attend "dates" with the Lord every morning, he heightens my awareness of His presence, building my confidence in Him and not myself.

For years, I requested the Lord to increase my love for Him. Today, because of our "dates," He has become my *Everything*. His abundant love flows over me each day. Through Him alone, I can find joy when I experience trials of various kinds because I know they perfect my faith in Him. (James 1:2-4)

This book is a workbook. The pages are your personal workspace. For six days your sessions are divided into three parts averaging five minutes to complete each section. *Day seven, rest in the wisdom received this week.* On day seven, you might attend your local church. Here you will participate in the three sessions with the body of Christ. As you meet with Him for six weeks, you will notice a sense of God's love and purpose, replacing your void.

My recommendation is to find a friend or maybe a small group to complete *A 15 Minute "Date" with God.* Starting a new routine is difficult to do on our own without accountability.

> *"Two are better than one because they have a good reward for their efforts. For if either falls, his companion can lift him up; but pity the one who falls without another to lift him up."*
>
> *-Ecclesiastes 4:9-10 (HCSB)*

So, find that person, who can partner with you for your accountability as you both walk through this study.

However, if right now you prefer to venture through this study alone, as I did, my prayer is that your time with God will be enriched. With every morning, you rise with anticipation driving your roots deep below the surface, so you complete the full 40 days.

How does it work?

Choose a book of the Bible you would like to study. Before you choose a Book of Scripture, seek the Author, and ask Him what you should read first.

> *"If any of you lacks wisdom, you should ask God, who gives generously to all without finding fault, and it will be given to you."*
>
> *- James 1:5 (NIV)*

Ask the Lord for wisdom on what Book of Scripture He prefers you to read first. God always points me in His direction. He has used Scriptures from sermons, the verse of the day sent to me from various Bible Apps or subscription emails, my local Christian radio stations, or Podcasts to help point me in His direction. If any reference of Scripture resonates with my spirit that becomes my new book to embark on next. Once I know which Book of Scripture God invites me to read, I begin to indulge.

My husband and I try to go on a "date" at least once a month. Every date, we find a place that serves dessert, hopefully containing chocolate. Oreo Cookies are one of my favorite desserts, especially the double stuffed Oreos. When I go on my date with the Lord every morning, I always have dessert. The breakdown of the 15 minute "Date" with God is like an Oreo cookie. There are three pieces to an Oreo cookie, and there are three sections to *A 15 Minute "Date" with God.*

The First 5 minutes (Pray)

When I wake in the morning, I acknowledge the Lord by stating, "Good morning, Lord." I open my prayer journal and begin communicating my need for God. Prayer recognizes our need that only God can fill. When we get out of the habit of praying daily, we falsely believe we achieved the blessing of the Lord all on our own. Prayer reminds us of who is really in control and what little we can control.

> *"Therefore let us approach the throne of grace with boldness, so that we may receive mercy and find grace to help us at the proper time."*
>
> *-Hebrews 4:16 (HCSB)*

Prayer also prepares our hearts to hear the Word of the Lord. When we humble ourselves by confessing with our mouth, He softens our hearts. God draws us near to hear His voice speak truth over us.

"God's there, listening for all who pray, for all who pray and mean it"

-Psalm 145:18 (MSG)

Prayer can be said out loud, in our heads, or on paper. I tend to do all three throughout my day. But for my 5 minutes when I'm on my date with the Lord, I journal. I choose to journal because it helps me focus and not ramble on, preventing my mind from spinning off in different directions. Journaling my prayers help me recall every place, every moment God has been faithful to me, building my confidence in the Lord. My prayer journals are our love story written on the pages from my heart.

The Second 5 minutes (Read)

My kids love the stuffing in their Oreo cookies. Scripture is the yummy, sweet stuffing in the center of our 3 (5 minutes) sessions.

> *For this 5-minute session, chose a Book of the Bible you would like to read from beginning to end.*

Remember, you're only reading for 5 minutes, so don't expect to complete a full book in one sitting. You might not even complete a whole chapter in the 5 minute time frame. That is alright!

> *"Remember, reading His Word is not about the AMOUNT of words you read but rather about the impact that those words have on you. This is why ONE or TWO verses are often better than many." -Priscilla Shirer [3]*

As you read, you will ask yourself questions. These questions are designed to help expand your thoughts and understanding of the text.

Maybe reading is not your favorite learning strategy. There are several free Bible Apps that will read the Scripture for you in whatever version of the text you prefer.

> *Use whatever method helps you digest Scripture.*

Five minutes isn't a long time to read and digest significant passages of Scripture, so keep it simple at first until you get the hang of it. Resist the urge to skip this activity. As I said, this is your stuffing, the sweet cream that holds the other two sections together.

> *If you skip this, the cookie will crumble and won't be as satisfying.*

The Final 5 Minutes (Praise)

Before the end of every date, it's good to thank your "date" for their time. The last 5 minutes with the Lord, I WORSHIP Him. When worshiping, my focus is on God alone. There is no agenda when I offer God my gifts of praise. He deserves all that I have.

> *"Shout for joy to the LORD, all the earth. Worship the LORD with gladness; come before him with joyful songs."*
>
> *-Psalm 100:1-2 (NIV)*

I love this verse because it doesn't state to offer your songs of worship on perfect pitch. It says, "shout for joy," sing with joy in your heart. There are many ways to glorify the Lord. Pick your favorite. I love to sing praises to my King, so worship music is the way I express my gratitude. Maybe you are a writer and prefer to write out your blessings like a "Thank you" card to the Lord. Perhaps you enjoy drawing an image that represents your adoration to the Lord; there is a Free Draw space after every third day. *Choose the method that works best for you. These five minutes are reserved for you to offer gratitude to the Lord any way you prefer.*

Pray, Read, and Praise are the three activities we'll focus on for the next 6 weeks as we attend our 15 minute "Dates" with God. Sounds easy, doesn't it? You might have doubts because this sounds so simple. Maybe you're thinking like my daughter that "fundamentals" are not the skills you need to refresh on.

But this study might surprise you. Before writing this book, I challenged my readers to use this 15 minute "Date" with God to engage in all three activities for 40 days. I was curious if they would experience the same richness in their own "dates" with God. Guess what... THEY DID!!!

> *"I am an 84-year-old woman who loves her Lord beyond. I have had Quiet Times and have done Ladies Bible Studies for years. This study has given me a new deeper connection with God. It shows us how to do Prayer Time, Bible Study, and Worship within our 15 minutes. I recommend it to all ladies, no matter how long you have been a Christian." – Peggy Brooks [11]*

Each lady, who chose to take the challenge, commented on how grateful they were for their "dates" with God. Their personal relationship with God grew intimate and mature. Scripture quenched their thirst as they were mesmerized by His wonders.

God is a God of abundance and He has no favorites. If He met with these ladies and me, transforming our relationship with Him, I believe He desires to form that kind of bond with you as well.

For the next six weeks, will you join God for a 15-minute Date?

1st Evaluation

Before you begin attending dates with God, here is a little evaluation to help you evaluate your intimacy with God. You will take this same evaluation at the end of the 6 weeks.

1. On a scale from 0 to 10, (0 being never and 10 being all the time): Where would you rate your relationship with God? How close are you with Him?

0	5	10

2. On a scale from 0 to 10, (0 being never and 10 being all the time): How often do you pray about offering Him glory, discussing choices, asking for His will to be done?

0	5	10

3. On a scale from 0 to 10, (0 being never and 10 being all the time): How often do you open His Word throughout your week?

0	5	10

4. On a scale from 0 to 10, (0 being never and 10 being all the time): How often do you seek for answers in God's Word?

0	5	10

5. On a scale from 0 to 10, (0 being never and 10 being all the time): How often do you sing or offer praise to the Lord for being such a good God?

0	5	10

Week One

Let's start simple. When rekindling or starting a new relationship, slow and steady helps keep the momentum. Jumping in too fast doesn't allow the process to happen naturally. Our heart is in the right place, but overexerting ourselves tends to smother the flame, causing burn out. Each week is designed to help keep a manageable pace to prevent burn out. Resources are provided to help you reach your goal while meeting for 15 minutes with the LORD.

We want to keep it simple and be mindful of your time. As you begin, set a timer for 5 minutes before you start each section to help you keep track of time. However, if a timer triggers anxiety and stress, keep it simple, and remember **THREE**.

"He brought us to this place and gave us this land, a land flowing with milk and honey; and now I bring the first fruits of the soil that you, LORD have given to me." Place the basket before the LORD your God and bow down before Him.

- Deuteronomy 26:9-10 (NIV)

As a kindergartener, I wished my last name was "Apple" since it started with "A," positioning me to stand in the front of the line. Being first is a yearning for everyone. There is a level of importance with the title of FIRST, placing a higher value on the one who holds that position.

God requires us to serve Him first, placing His value above our own. The Father sacrificed His Firstborn Son for us, bestowing His first for us. He mandates reciprocation, nothing more nothing less.

But do we surrender our best, our first for Him?

Yielding our first before the LORD is not a characteristic of the world. Relinquishing our first is a piece of the puzzle that helps us not conform to this world. But to offer God our best, first means more than money or gifts. Presenting Him with our first is much deeper than our provisions.

The first command of the Ten Commandments is to "Love your God with all your heart and with all your soul," making Him FIRST in our lives. God wants to be our First thoughts, involved in our Firsts moments, and be our First love.

We know this in our heads, so how can we acknowledge it in our hearts?

It's not natural for us to serve someone other than ourselves. We must train our head knowledge to alter our heart knowledge. So here is a challenge for 40 Days: will you offer your **FIRST** 15 minutes of your day to the Lord?

God is faithful to meet with us. And I believe His promise that His Word will not return void. *Will you give Him your first 15 minutes today for the next 40 Days?*

Step 1: PRAY- Jesus valued prayer and taught his disciples the Seven ways to seek the Lord in prayer, called the "The Lord's Prayer." *(Matthew 6:9-13)*

The template for this section gives a format example with space for personalized requests in modern-day language. Remember this week is about learning moderation, so even though there are seven elements of this prayer, it does not mean you are expected to complete all seven every day. Five minutes allows you to pray through at least three sections.

Pray 1-3 of the 7 ways to seek the Lord in prayer.

1. *Seek and Acknowledge who God is*
2. *Seek God's will*
3. *Seek God's provision*
4. *Seek God's forgiveness*
5. *Seek to forgive others*
6. *Seek God in times of trials*
7. *Seek God to claim victory over the evil one*

Step 2: READ- Choose one book of the Bible you would like to read entirely. Begin reading Chapter 1:1-3 (read THREE passages) *and complete the questions located under step 2 after reading your passage to help expand your understanding.*

Step 3: PRAISE- Play one song or write a "Thank you" letter to the Lord for all that He has done. Remember, it doesn't matter if you sing off-key; God wants to hear your joyful song! If you choose to sing your praises today, write the name of the song in the worship box to remember the joy placed in your heart for Him.

The templates are designed to help you stay focused on your talking points with God. Each week will supply you with a new template for the next six days. Use them, write on them, draw on them, and explore with them. Dig as deep as you would like to go. Supportive resources are in the back of the book for your enjoyment. These resources consist of names of God, a list of concordance, and useful websites that have helped me. The design of this study offers you the freedom to decide how deep you want to go.

Whatever you put in is what you will get out of this study. So, are you in? Are you ready to receive your fresh manna from the Lord every day? Pour yourself a cup of coffee or a glass of your favorite morning beverage and begin…

DAY 1: Step 1- PRAY

Date: _____

Good morning _____,

1. Holy, Holy, Holy are you, Lord God Almighty. You are:

2. Lord, my flesh craves

_____

_____

but I surrender to Your will and Your way. Father, I pray not my will but YOURS be done. Increase my faith to trust you with this.

3. You are the Alpha and Omega. Thank you for going before me and standing behind me. You know all my needs. Lord, you never fail to provide everything I need. Father, here is a need I lay at your feet...

4. God, there is no other god but you. Father forgive me for forgetting this truth in my actions. Forgive me for serving my selfish desires. Lord, here are my sins and my struggles. I acknowledge them before you, please forgive me for...

5. Father, I struggle to forgive others who have caused me great pain. Lord, help me forgive them as you have forgiven me. Bring to my mind someone I need to forgive and then help me to follow through...

6. Heavenly Father, you are a good Father and every test is for my good. Lord, help me trust you during this trial and remember Your faithfulness. Help me as I face

_____

_____

_____ I pray Father, for your faithful strength to help me stand firm in my faith. I pray you remind me that in every storm, you are working all things for my good. I ask for peace that surpasses all my understanding as we walk through this together.

7. Lord, in you alone is where I find my victory with the enemy. Father, I ask for your armor to cover me. And by your Son's name I claim victory and the enemy must flee. I pray in the name of Jesus, Devil you must leave:

Father, thank you for the people I'm blessed to love. Lord, I place

_____

_____

_____

_____in your hands.

Father help me love my neighbors as You love them. Father, please help...

Free space to add any other requests...

Lord before I open Your Word, I ask you to open my eyes to see what YOU want to reveal to me today.

In the precious name of Jesus I pray all these things,

_____.

Step 2: READ

Scripture read today: _____

What does this passage show me about God's character?
God is faithful to His promises. What promise did you read about today?
What numbers did I see in the Scripture? Why was that detail mentioned?
What word or phrases stood out to me and why?
What word/s do I need to look up the meaning?
List the name of the town mentioned in the passage. Later, when you have more time, google that name. Some Biblical town names have a different name today. What do I know about that town? Have these places been mentioned in another passage of Scripture?
What did I glean from this passage that I need to implement in my life? Take a minute to ask the Lord to help you implement these areas in your life.

Step 3: PRAISE

All about Worship: Worship is merely praising the Lord for being God. Giving thanks and glory to the King of kings. On this page either write, sing, or find some way to show the God of all Creation gratitude for who He is to you. Thank Him for your breath, your life, providing everything you need, and for being a good good Father.

Worship Musical Group Albums recommended:

Lauren Daigle— Look up child

Mercy Me– Almost There

Bethel Music– You Make Me Brave, Victory (Live)

I am They– I am They

Passion– Follow you Anywhere

Hillsong Worship

Toby Mac– The Elements

Meredith Andrews– Worth it All

Chris McClarney—Breakthrough (Live)

Danny Gokey– Haven't Seen it Yet

Various Artists– Your Reckless Love

Rend Collective– The Art of Celebration

Mandisa– Overcomer, What If we were Real, Out of the Dark

Shane & Shane

Tauren Wells

Or google Christian Radio and choose your favorite station and listen to a song or two for the next five minutes. If you like to write your praise down, here is a space for you. If you sing a song, write the title of the song in the box to help you remember the joy you found today.

DAY 2: Step 1- PRAY

Date: _____

Good morning _____,

1. *Holy, Holy, Holy are you, Lord God Almighty. You are:*

2. Lord, my flesh craves

_____

_____

but I surrender to Your will and Your way. Father, I pray not my will but YOURS be done. Increase my faith to trust you with this.

3. You are the Alpha and Omega. Thank you for going before me and standing behind me. You know all my needs. Lord, you never fail to provide everything I need. Father, here is a need I lay at your feet...

4. God, there is no other god but you. Father forgive me for forgetting this truth in my actions. Forgive me for serving my selfish desires. Lord, here are my sins and my struggles. I acknowledge them before you, please forgive me for...

5. Father, I struggle to forgive others who have caused me great pain. Lord, help me forgive them as you have forgiven me. Bring to my mind someone I need to forgive and then help me to follow through...

6. Heavenly Father, you are a good Father and every test is for my good. Lord, help me trust you during this trial and remember Your faithfulness. Help me as I face

_____

_____

_____ I pray Father, for your faithful strength to help me stand firm in my faith. I pray you remind me that in every storm, you are working all things for my good. I ask for peace that surpasses all my understanding as we walk through this together.

7. Lord, in you alone is where I find my victory with the enemy. Father, I ask for your armor to cover me. And by your Son's name I claim victory and the enemy must flee. I pray in the name of Jesus, Devil you must leave:

Father, thank you for the people I'm blessed to love. Lord, I place

_____

_____

_____

_____in your hands.

Father help me love my neighbors as You love them. Father, please help...

Free space to add any other requests...

Lord before I open Your Word, I ask you to open my eyes to see what YOU want to reveal to me today.

In the precious name of Jesus I pray all these things,

_____.

Step 2: READ

Scripture read today: _____

What does this passage show me about God's character?
God is faithful to His promises. What promise did you read about today?
What numbers did I see in the Scripture? Why was that detail mentioned?
What word or phrases stood out to me and why?
What word/s do I need to look up the meaning?
List the name of the town mentioned in the passage. Later, when you have more time, google that name. Some Biblical town names have a different name today. What do I know about that town? Have these places been mentioned in another passage of Scripture?
What did I glean from this passage that I need to implement in my life? Take a minute to ask the Lord to help you implement these areas in your life.

Step 3: PRAISE

All about Worship: Worship is merely praising the Lord for being God. Giving thanks and glory to the King of kings. On this page either write, sing, or find some way to show the God of all Creation gratitude for who He is to you. Thank Him for your breath, your life, providing everything you need, and for being a good good Father.

Worship Musical Group Albums recommended:

Lauren Daigle— Look up child

Mercy Me– Almost There

Bethel Music– You Make Me Brave, Victory (Live)

I am They– I am They

Passion– Follow you Anywhere

Hillsong Worship

Toby Mac– The Elements

Meredith Andrews– Worth it All

Chris McClarney—Breakthrough (Live)

Danny Gokey– Haven't Seen it Yet

Various Artists– Your Reckless Love

Rend Collective– The Art of Celebration

Mandisa– Overcomer, What If we were Real, Out of the Dark

Shane & Shane

Tauren Wells

Or google Christian Radio and choose your favorite station and listen to a song or two for the next five minutes. If you like to write your praise down, here is a space for you. If you sing a song, write the title of the song in the box to help you remember the joy you found today.

DAY 3: Step 1- PRAY

Date_____

Good morning _____,

1. Holy, Holy, Holy are you, Lord God Almighty. You are:

2. Lord, my flesh craves

_____

_____

but I surrender to Your will and Your way. Father, I pray not my will but YOURS be done. Increase my faith to trust you with this.

3. You are the Alpha and Omega. Thank you for going before me and standing behind me. You know all my needs. Lord, you never fail to provide everything I need. Father, here is a need I lay at your feet...

4. God, there is no other god but you. Father forgive me for forgetting this truth in my actions. Forgive me for serving my selfish desires. Lord, here are my sins and my struggles. I acknowledge them before you, please forgive me for...

5. Father, I struggle to forgive others who have caused me great pain. Lord, help me forgive them as you have forgiven me. Bring to my mind someone I need to forgive and then help me to follow through...

6. Heavenly Father, you are a good Father and every test is for my good. Lord, help me trust you during this trial and remember Your faithfulness. Help me as I face

_____

_____

_____ I pray Father, for your faithful

strength to help me stand firm in my faith. I pray you remind me that in every storm, you are working all things for my good. I ask for peace that surpasses all my understanding as we walk through this together.

7. Lord, in you alone is where I find my victory with the enemy. Father, I ask for your armor to cover me. And by your Son's name I claim victory and the enemy must flee. I pray in the name of Jesus, Devil you must leave:

Father, thank you for the people I'm blessed to love. Lord, I place

_____

_____

_____

_____in your hands.

Father help me love my neighbors as You love them. Father, please help...

Free space to add any other requests...

Lord before I open Your Word, I ask you to open my eyes to see what YOU want to reveal to me today.

In the precious name of Jesus I pray all these things,

_____.

Step 2: READ

Scripture read today: _____

What does this passage show me about God's character?

God is faithful to His promises. What promise did you read about today?

What numbers did I see in the Scripture? Why was that detail mentioned?

What word or phrases stood out to me and why?

What word/s do I need to look up the meaning?

List the name of the town mentioned in the passage. Later, when you have more time, google that name. Some Biblical town names have a different name today. What do I know about that town? Have these places been mentioned in another passage of Scripture?

What did I glean from this passage that I need to implement in my life? Take a minute to ask the Lord to help you implement these areas in your life.

Step 3: PRAISE

All about Worship: Worship is merely praising the Lord for being God. Giving thanks and glory to the King of kings. On this page either write, sing, or find some way to show the God of all Creation gratitude for who He is to you. Thank Him for your breath, your life, providing everything you need, and for being a good good Father.

Worship Musical Group Albums recommended:

Lauren Daigle— Look up child

Mercy Me– Almost There

Bethel Music– You Make Me Brave, Victory (Live)

I am They– I am They

Passion– Follow you Anywhere

Hillsong Worship

Toby Mac– The Elements

Meredith Andrews– Worth it All

Chris McClarney—Breakthrough (Live)

Danny Gokey– Haven't Seen it Yet

Various Artists– Your Reckless Love

Rend Collective– The Art of Celebration

Mandisa– Overcomer, What If we were Real, Out of the Dark

Shane & Shane

Tauren Wells

Or google Christian Radio and choose your favorite station and listen to a song or two for the next five minutes. If you like to write your praise down, here is a space for you. If you sing a song, write the title of the song in the box to help you remember the joy you found today.

FIRST [5]

Before I bring my need, I will bring my heart
Before I lift my cares, I will lift my arms
I wanna know You, I wanna find You
In every season, in every moment
Before I bring my need, I will bring my heart
And seek You
First
I wanna seek You, I wanna seek You
First
I wanna keep You, I wanna keep You
First
More than anything I want, I want You
First
Before I speak a word, let me hear Your voice
And in the midst of pain, let me feel Your joy, ooh
I wanna know You, I wanna find You
In every season, in every moment
Before I speak a word, I will bring my heart
And seek You
First
You are my treasure and my reward
Let nothing ever come before
You are my treasure and my reward
Let nothing ever come before
I seek You
First
I wanna seek You, seek You, seek You
First
I wanna keep You, I wanna keep You
First
More than anything I want, I want You
First
First

Songwriters: Jason Ingram / Paul Mabury / Mia Fieldes / Lauren Daigle / Charles Bentley

First lyrics © Essential Music Publishing, Capitol Christian Music Group

Free Draw

This space is for you to illustrate your week, what you are learning, ways God is speaking to you, or maybe draw an image God used to say, "I love YOU."

DAY 4: Step 1- PRAY

Date: _____

Good morning _____,

1. *Holy, Holy, Holy are you, Lord God Almighty. You are:*

2. *Lord, my flesh craves*

_____

_____

but I surrender to Your will and Your way. Father, I pray not my will but YOURS be done. Increase my faith to trust you with this.

3. *You are the Alpha and Omega. Thank you for going before me and standing behind me. You know all my needs. Lord, you never fail to provide everything I need. Father, here is a need I lay at your feet...*

4. *God, there is no other god but you. Father forgive me for forgetting this truth in my actions. Forgive me for serving my selfish desires. Lord, here are my sins and my struggles. I acknowledge them before you, please forgive me for...*

5. *Father, I struggle to forgive others who have caused me great pain. Lord, help me forgive them as you have forgiven me. Bring to my mind someone I need to forgive and then help me to follow through...*

6. *Heavenly Father, you are a good Father and every test is for my good. Lord, help me trust you during this trial and remember Your faithfulness. Help me as I face*

_____

_____

_____ *I pray Father, for your faithful*

strength to help me stand firm in my faith. I pray you remind me that in every storm, you are working all things for my good. I ask for peace that surpasses all my understanding as we walk through this together.

7. *Lord, in you alone is where I find my victory with the enemy. Father, I ask for your armor to cover me. And by your Son's name I claim victory and the enemy must flee. I pray in the name of Jesus, Devil you must leave:*

Father, thank you for the people I'm blessed to love. Lord, I place

_____

_____

_____

_____ *in your hands.*

Father help me love my neighbors as You love them. Father, please help...

Free space to add any other requests...

Lord before I open Your Word, I ask you to open my eyes to see what YOU want to reveal to me today.

In the precious name of Jesus I pray all these things,

_____ .

Step 2: READ

Scripture read today: _____

What does this passage show me about God's character?

God is faithful to His promises. What promise did you read about today?

What numbers did I see in the Scripture? Why was that detail mentioned?

What word or phrases stood out to me and why?

What word/s do I need to look up the meaning?

List the name of the town mentioned in the passage. Later, when you have more time, google that name. Some Biblical town names have a different name today. What do I know about that town? Have these places been mentioned in another passage of Scripture?

What did I glean from this passage that I need to implement in my life? Take a minute to ask the Lord to help you implement these areas in your life.

Step 3: PRAISE

All about Worship: Worship is merely praising the Lord for being God. Giving thanks and glory to the King of kings. On this page either write, sing, or find some way to show the God of all Creation gratitude for who He is to you. Thank Him for your breath, your life, providing everything you need, and for being a good good Father.

Worship Musical Group Albums recommended:

Lauren Daigle— Look up child

Mercy Me– Almost There

Bethel Music– You Make Me Brave, Victory (Live)

I am They– I am They

Passion– Follow you Anywhere

Hillsong Worship

Toby Mac– The Elements

Meredith Andrews– Worth it All

Chris McClarney—Breakthrough (Live)

Danny Gokey– Haven't Seen it Yet

Various Artists– Your Reckless Love

Rend Collective– The Art of Celebration

Mandisa– Overcomer, What If we were Real, Out of the Dark

Shane & Shane

Tauren Wells

Or google Christian Radio and choose your favorite station and listen to a song or two for the next five minutes. If you like to write your praise down, here is a space for you. If you sing a song, write the title of the song in the box to help you remember the joy you found today.

DAY 5: Step 1- PRAY

Date: _____

Good morning _____ ,

1. Holy, Holy, Holy are you, Lord God Almighty. You are:

2. Lord, my flesh craves

_____

_____

but I surrender to Your will and Your way. Father, I pray not my will but YOURS be done. Increase my faith to trust you with this.

3. You are the Alpha and Omega. Thank you for going before me and standing behind me. You know all my needs. Lord, you never fail to provide everything I need. Father, here is a need I lay at your feet...

4. God, there is no other god but you. Father forgive me for forgetting this truth in my actions. Forgive me for serving my selfish desires. Lord, here are my sins and my struggles. I acknowledge them before you, please forgive me for...

5. Father, I struggle to forgive others who have caused me great pain. Lord, help me forgive them as you have forgiven me. Bring to my mind someone I need to forgive and then help me to follow through...

6. Heavenly Father, you are a good Father and every test is for my good. Lord, help me trust you during this trial and remember Your faithfulness. Help me as I face

_____

_____

_____ I pray Father, for your faithful strength to help me stand firm in my faith. I pray you remind me that in every storm, you are working all things for my good. I ask for peace that surpasses all my understanding as we walk through this together.

7. Lord, in you alone is where I find my victory with the enemy. Father, I ask for your armor to cover me. And by your Son's name I claim victory and the enemy must flee. I pray in the name of Jesus, Devil you must leave:

Father, thank you for the people I'm blessed to love. Lord, I place

_____

_____

_____

_____in your hands.

Father help me love my neighbors as You love them. Father, please help...

Free space to add any other requests...

Lord before I open Your Word, I ask you to open my eyes to see what YOU want to reveal to me today.

In the precious name of Jesus I pray all these things,

_____.

Step 2: READ

Scripture read today: _____

What does this passage show me about God's character?

God is faithful to His promises. What promise did you read about today?

What numbers did I see in the Scripture? Why was that detail mentioned?

What word or phrases stood out to me and why?

What word/s do I need to look up the meaning?

List the name of the town mentioned in the passage. Later, when you have more time, google that name. Some Biblical town names have a different name today. What do I know about that town? Have these places been mentioned in another passage of Scripture?

What did I glean from this passage that I need to implement in my life? Take a minute to ask the Lord to help you implement these areas in your life.

Step 3: PRAISE

All about Worship: Worship is merely praising the Lord for being God. Giving thanks and glory to the King of kings. On this page either write, sing, or find some way to show the God of all Creation gratitude for who He is to you. Thank Him for your breath, your life, providing everything you need, and for being a good good Father.

Worship Musical Group Albums recommended:

Lauren Daigle— Look up child

Mercy Me– Almost There

Bethel Music– You Make Me Brave, Victory (Live)

I am They– I am They

Passion– Follow you Anywhere

Hillsong Worship

Toby Mac– The Elements

Meredith Andrews– Worth it All

Chris McClarney—Breakthrough (Live)

Danny Gokey– Haven't Seen it Yet

Various Artists– Your Reckless Love

Rend Collective– The Art of Celebration

Mandisa– Overcomer, What If we were Real, Out of the Dark

Shane & Shane

Tauren Wells

Or google Christian Radio and choose your favorite station and listen to a song or two for the next five minutes. If you like to write your praise down, here is a space for you. If you sing a song, write the title of the song in the box to help you remember the joy you found today.

DAY 6: Step 1- PRAY

Date: _____

Good morning _____,

1. Holy, Holy, Holy are you, Lord God Almighty. You are:

2. Lord, my flesh craves

_____

_____

but I surrender to Your will and Your way. Father, I pray not my will but YOURS be done. Increase my faith to trust you with this.

3. You are the Alpha and Omega. Thank you for going before me and standing behind me. You know all my needs. Lord, you never fail to provide everything I need. Father, here is a need I lay at your feet...

4. God, there is no other god but you. Father forgive me for forgetting this truth in my actions. Forgive me for serving my selfish desires. Lord, here are my sins and my struggles. I acknowledge them before you, please forgive me for...

5. Father, I struggle to forgive others who have caused me great pain. Lord, help me forgive them as you have forgiven me. Bring to my mind someone I need to forgive and then help me to follow through...

6. Heavenly Father, you are a good Father and every test is for my good. Lord, help me trust you during this trial and remember Your faithfulness. Help me as I face

_____

_____

_____ I pray Father, for your faithful strength to help me stand firm in my faith. I pray you remind me that in every storm, you are working all things for my good. I ask for peace that surpasses all my understanding as we walk through this together.

7. Lord, in you alone is where I find my victory with the enemy. Father, I ask for your armor to cover me. And by your Son's name I claim victory and the enemy must flee. I pray in the name of Jesus, Devil you must leave:

Father, thank you for the people I'm blessed to love. Lord, I place

_____

_____

_____

_____in your hands.

Father help me love my neighbors as You love them. Father, please help...

Free space to add any other requests...

Lord before I open Your Word, I ask you to open my eyes to see what YOU want to reveal to me today.

In the precious name of Jesus I pray all these things,

_____.

Step 2: READ

Scripture read today: _____

What does this passage show me about God's character?

God is faithful to His promises. What promise did you read about today?

What numbers did I see in the Scripture? Why was that detail mentioned?

What word or phrases stood out to me and why?

What word/s do I need to look up the meaning?

List the name of the town mentioned in the passage. Later, when you have more time, google that name. Some Biblical town names have a different name today. What do I know about that town? Have these places been mentioned in another passage of Scripture?

What did I glean from this passage that I need to implement in my life? Take a minute to ask the Lord to help you implement these areas in your life.

Step 3: PRAISE

All about Worship: Worship is merely praising the Lord for being God. Giving thanks and glory to the King of kings. On this page either write, sing, or find some way to show the God of all Creation gratitude for who He is to you. Thank Him for your breath, your life, providing everything you need, and for being a good good Father.

Worship Musical Group Albums recommended:

Lauren Daigle— Look up child

Mercy Me– Almost There

Bethel Music– You Make Me Brave, Victory (Live)

I am They– I am They

Passion– Follow you Anywhere

Hillsong Worship

Toby Mac– The Elements

Meredith Andrews– Worth it All

Chris McClarney—Breakthrough (Live)

Danny Gokey– Haven't Seen it Yet

Various Artists– Your Reckless Love

Rend Collective– The Art of Celebration

Mandisa– Overcomer, What If we were Real, Out of the Dark

Shane & Shane

Tauren Wells

Or google Christian Radio and choose your favorite station and listen to a song or two for the next five minutes. If you like to write your praise down, here is a space for you. If you sing a song, write the title of the song in the box to help you remember the joy you found today.

Week Two

So, how did you do? Were you able to complete all <u>THREE</u> activities each day? Don't fret about slip-ups but make corrections to stay on course. New habits take time to become routines. Give yourself grace. God delights in our choice to spend the first 15 minutes of our day with Him.

> *The LORD makes firm the steps of the one who delights in him; though he may stumble, he will not fall, for the LORD upholds him with his hand.*
>
> *-Psalm 37:23-24 (NIV)*

The struggle is real to adjust from living for self to living for Him. When my alarm sounds before the sun wakes, that temptation to hit snooze and to stay in bed creeps in. I fight this battle by picturing the Lord beckoning me to come visit with Him. This image of the LORD desiring time with ME stirs my heartstrings, prompting my body to emerge from the sheets.

In those moments with Him, God lavishes on us REAL love, His love. As we continue with our stride, the Lord is cheering us on, guiding us to the next secure step along His path. As the Alpha and Omega (the beginning and the end), God promises to make firm His steps as He goes before us and to catch us when we stumble.

And there are moments we need His hand. Without condemnation in His eyes, He offers to help us stand. His mercy is new, revealed every morning as the Sun rises. With each new day, we place faith in the wisdom that God is always for us. As we continue to seek Him first every morning, The Holy Spirit will open our eyes to how He sees, transforming our hearts to beat with His.

The enemy will try to distract you, make you exhausted, or jam your schedule with other things you need to accomplish for the day. His goal is to keep you away from God. The enemy knows the plans God orchestrates are for your good. The enemy fears our transformation. He knows as you press into God, you begin to transform into the warrior God designed you to be. So, resist those temptations!

A way for you to protect yourself from the evil one's schemes is by placing the armor of God on daily. Starting your day with a 15 minute "Date" with God helps secure your armor for the day before you step out on the battlefield called life.

> *"So use every piece of God's armor to resist the enemy whenever he attacks, and when it is all over, you will still be standing up. But to do this, you will need the strong belt of truth and the breastplate of God's approval. Wear shoes that are able to speed you on as you preach the Good News of peace with God. In every battle you will need faith as your shield to stop the fiery arrows aimed at you by Satan. And you will need the helmet of salvation and the sword of the Spirit—*

which is the Word of God. Pray all the time. Ask God for anything in line with the Holy Spirit's wishes. Plead with him, reminding him of your needs, and keep praying earnestly for all Christians everywhere.

-Ephesians 6: 13-18 (TLB)

Stand firm in your commitment to God! Remember, it's only a 15-minute Date.

Step 1: PRAY– *This week, we will still be praying through 1-3 of* the 7 ways to seek the Lord in prayer. If you would like to press on with some of the others after you have prayed 1-3, feel free to continue as long as time permits. Remember, we're working on maintaining our pace and trying to stick with our 5-minute routine.

1. *Seek and Acknowledge who God is*

2. *Seek God's will*

3. *Seek God's provision*

4. *Seek God's forgiveness*

5. *Seek to forgive others*

6. *Seek God in times of trials*

7. *Seek God to claim victory over the evil one*

Step 2: READ– I hope you're enjoying the book of Scripture you have chosen. Remember, the goal is to complete a full book before starting a new one. Use your time to read and meditate on the passage throughout your day. R*ead three passages of one chapter and answer the questions on* the chapter in the book of your choice. Are you noticing some common character traits of God as you read? Do you see His promises written for you?

Step 3: PRAISE– The power of worship astonishes me. On a horrible day, a song will randomly play on the radio, altering my focus off of myself and the situation, illuminating the goodness of the Lord. Worship lifts my eyes to the heavens, and my fears melt away as I praise God for who He is and what He has done. This week, if God places a song in your heart, write the lyrics down. Be intentional and listen to the message. God is speaking to you through His song.

Remember, the templates are designed to help you stay on task as you talk with God. Keep your answers simple. Don't let them stress you out. If you're running out of space to write, then you might want to purchase a cheap spiral notebook. If you're going to dig deeper, use the resources in the back of the book. The design of this study offers you the freedom to decide how deep you want to go.

Whatever you put in is what you will get out of this study. Are you ready to receive your fresh manna from the Lord every day? Let's begin…

DAY 1: Step 1- PRAY

Date: _____

Good morning _____,

1. Holy, Holy, Holy are you, Lord God Almighty. You are:

2. Lord, my flesh craves

_____

_____

but I surrender to Your will and Your way. Father, I pray not my will but YOURS be done. Increase my faith to trust you with this.

3. You are the Alpha and Omega. Thank you for going before me and standing behind me. You know all my needs. Lord, you never fail to provide everything I need. Father, here is a need I lay at your feet...

4. God, there is no other god but you. Father forgive me for forgetting this truth in my actions. Forgive me for serving my selfish desires. Lord, here are my sins and my struggles. I acknowledge them before you, please forgive me for...

5. Father, I struggle to forgive others who have caused me great pain. Lord, help me forgive them as you have forgiven me. Bring to my mind someone I need to forgive and then help me to follow through...

6. Heavenly Father, you are a good Father and every test is for my good. Lord, help me trust you during this trial and remember Your faithfulness. Help me as I face

_____

_____

_____ I pray Father, for your faithful strength to help me stand firm in my faith. I pray you remind me that in every storm, you are working all things for my good. I ask for peace that surpasses all my understanding as we walk through this together.

7. Lord, in you alone is where I find my victory with the enemy. Father, I ask for your armor to cover me. And by your Son's name I claim victory and the enemy must flee. I pray in the name of Jesus, Devil you must leave:

Father, thank you for the people I'm blessed to love. Lord, I place

_____

_____

_____

_____in your hands.

Father help me love my neighbors as You love them. Father, please help...

Free space to add any other requests...

Lord before I open Your Word, I ask you to open my eyes to see what YOU want to reveal to me today.

In the precious name of Jesus I pray all these things,

_____.

Step 2: READ

Scripture read today: _____

What does this passage show me about God's character?

God is faithful to His promises. What promise did you read about today?

What numbers did I see in the Scripture? Why was that detail mentioned?

What word or phrases stood out to me and why?

What word/s do I need to look up the meaning?

List the name of the town mentioned in the passage. Later, when you have more time, google that name. Some Biblical town names have a different name today. What do I know about that town? Have these places been mentioned in another passage of Scripture?

What did I glean from this passage that I need to implement in my life? Take a minute to ask the Lord to help you implement these areas in your life.

Step 3: PRAISE

All about Worship: Worship is merely praising the Lord for being God. Giving thanks and glory to the King of kings. On this page either write, sing, or find some way to show the God of all Creation gratitude for who He is to you. Thank Him for your breath, your life, providing everything you need, and for being a good good Father.

Worship Musical Group Albums recommended:

Lauren Daigle— Look up child

Mercy Me– Almost There

Bethel Music– You Make Me Brave, Victory (Live)

I am They– I am They

Passion– Follow you Anywhere

Hillsong Worship

Toby Mac– The Elements

Meredith Andrews– Worth it All

Chris McClarney—Breakthrough (Live)

Danny Gokey– Haven't Seen it Yet

Various Artists– Your Reckless Love

Rend Collective– The Art of Celebration

Mandisa– Overcomer, What If we were Real, Out of the Dark

Shane & Shane

Tauren Wells

Or google Christian Radio and choose your favorite station and listen to a song or two for the next five minutes. If you like to write your praise down, here is a space for you. If you sing a song, write the title of the song in the box to help you remember the joy you found today.

DAY 2: Step 1- PRAY

Date: _____

Good morning _____,

1. Holy, Holy, Holy are you, Lord God Almighty. You are:

2. Lord, my flesh craves

_____

_____

but I surrender to Your will and Your way. Father, I pray not my will but YOURS be done. Increase my faith to trust you with this.

3. You are the Alpha and Omega. Thank you for going before me and standing behind me. You know all my needs. Lord, you never fail to provide everything I need. Father, here is a need I lay at your feet...

4. God, there is no other god but you. Father forgive me for forgetting this truth in my actions. Forgive me for serving my selfish desires. Lord, here are my sins and my struggles. I acknowledge them before you, please forgive me for...

5. Father, I struggle to forgive others who have caused me great pain. Lord, help me forgive them as you have forgiven me. Bring to my mind someone I need to forgive and then help me to follow through...

6. Heavenly Father, you are a good Father and every test is for my good. Lord, help me trust you during this trial and remember Your faithfulness. Help me as I face

_____

_____

_____ I pray Father, for your faithful strength to help me stand firm in my faith. I pray you remind me that in every storm, you are working all things for my good. I ask for peace that surpasses all my understanding as we walk through this together.

7. Lord, in you alone is where I find my victory with the enemy. Father, I ask for your armor to cover me. And by your Son's name I claim victory and the enemy must flee. I pray in the name of Jesus, Devil you must leave:

Father, thank you for the people I'm blessed to love. Lord, I place

_____

_____

_____

_____in your hands.

Father help me love my neighbors as You love them. Father, please help...

Free space to add any other requests...

Lord before I open Your Word, I ask you to open my eyes to see what YOU want to reveal to me today.

In the precious name of Jesus I pray all these things,

_____.

Step 2: READ

Scripture read today: _____

What does this passage show me about God's character?

God is faithful to His promises. What promise did you read about today?

What numbers did I see in the Scripture? Why was that detail mentioned?

What word or phrases stood out to me and why?

What word/s do I need to look up the meaning?

List the name of the town mentioned in the passage. Later, when you have more time, google that name. Some Biblical town names have a different name today. What do I know about that town? Have these places been mentioned in another passage of Scripture?

What did I glean from this passage that I need to implement in my life? Take a minute to ask the Lord to help you implement these areas in your life.

Step 3: PRAISE

All about Worship: Worship is merely praising the Lord for being God. Giving thanks and glory to the King of kings. On this page either write, sing, or find some way to show the God of all Creation gratitude for who He is to you. Thank Him for your breath, your life, providing everything you need, and for being a good good Father.

Worship Musical Group Albums recommended:

Lauren Daigle— Look up child

Mercy Me– Almost There

Bethel Music– You Make Me Brave, Victory (Live)

I am They– I am They

Passion– Follow you Anywhere

Hillsong Worship

Toby Mac– The Elements

Meredith Andrews– Worth it All

Chris McClarney—Breakthrough (Live)

Danny Gokey– Haven't Seen it Yet

Various Artists– Your Reckless Love

Rend Collective– The Art of Celebration

Mandisa– Overcomer, What If we were Real, Out of the Dark

Shane & Shane

Tauren Wells

Or google Christian Radio and choose your favorite station and listen to a song or two for the next five minutes. If you like to write your praise down, here is a space for you. If you sing a song, write the title of the song in the box to help you remember the joy you found today.

DAY 3: Step 1- PRAY

Date: _____

Good morning _____,

1. *Holy, Holy, Holy are you, Lord God Almighty. You are:*

2. *Lord, my flesh craves*

_____

_____

but I surrender to Your will and Your way. Father, I pray not my will but YOURS be done. Increase my faith to trust you with this.

3. *You are the Alpha and Omega. Thank you for going before me and standing behind me. You know all my needs. Lord, you never fail to provide everything I need. Father, here is a need I lay at your feet...*

4. *God, there is no other god but you. Father forgive me for forgetting this truth in my actions. Forgive me for serving my selfish desires. Lord, here are my sins and my struggles. I acknowledge them before you, please forgive me for...*

5. *Father, I struggle to forgive others who have caused me great pain. Lord, help me forgive them as you have forgiven me. Bring to my mind someone I need to forgive and then help me to follow through...*

6. Heavenly Father, you are a good Father and every test is for my good. Lord, help me trust you during this trial and remember Your faithfulness. Help me as I face

_____

_____

_____ I pray Father, for your faithful

strength to help me stand firm in my faith. I pray you remind me that in every storm, you are working all things for my good. I ask for peace that surpasses all my understanding as we walk through this together.

7. Lord, in you alone is where I find my victory with the enemy. Father, I ask for your armor to cover me. And by your Son's name I claim victory and the enemy must flee. I pray in the name of Jesus, Devil you must leave:

Father, thank you for the people I'm blessed to love. Lord, I place

_____

_____

_____

_____in your hands.

Father help me love my neighbors as You love them. Father, please help...

Free space to add any other requests...

Lord before I open Your Word, I ask you to open my eyes to see what YOU want to reveal to me today.

In the precious name of Jesus I pray all these things,

_____.

Step 2: READ

Scripture read today: _____

What does this passage show me about God's character?

God is faithful to His promises. What promise did you read about today?

What numbers did I see in the Scripture? Why was that detail mentioned?

What word or phrases stood out to me and why?

What word/s do I need to look up the meaning?

List the name of the town mentioned in the passage. Later, when you have more time, google that name. Some Biblical town names have a different name today. What do I know about that town? Have these places been mentioned in another passage of Scripture?

What did I glean from this passage that I need to implement in my life? Take a minute to ask the Lord to help you implement these areas in your life.

Step 3: PRAISE

All about Worship: Worship is merely praising the Lord for being God. Giving thanks and glory to the King of kings. On this page either write, sing, or find some way to show the God of all Creation gratitude for who He is to you. Thank Him for your breath, your life, providing everything you need, and for being a good good Father.

Worship Musical Group Albums recommended:

Lauren Daigle— Look up child

Mercy Me– Almost There

Bethel Music– You Make Me Brave, Victory (Live)

I am They– I am They

Passion– Follow you Anywhere

Hillsong Worship

Toby Mac– The Elements

Meredith Andrews– Worth it All

Chris McClarney—Breakthrough (Live)

Danny Gokey– Haven't Seen it Yet

Various Artists– Your Reckless Love

Rend Collective– The Art of Celebration

Mandisa– Overcomer, What If we were Real, Out of the Dark

Shane & Shane

Tauren Wells

Or google Christian Radio and choose your favorite station and listen to a song or two for the next five minutes. If you like to write your praise down, here is a space for you. If you sing a song, write the title of the song in the box to help you remember the joy you found today.

Spirit of the Living God [6]

Spirit of the Living God
Spirit of the Living God
We only wanna hear your voice
We're hanging on every word
Spirit of the Living God
Spirit of the Living God
We wanna know you more and more
We're hanging on every word
Speak to us
Spirit of the Living God
Spirit of the Living God
We're leaning in to all you are
Everything else can wait
Spirit of the Living God
Spirit of the Living God
Come now and breathe upon our hearts
Come now and have your way
Cause when you speak, when you move
When you do what only you can do
It changes us, it changes
What we see and what we seek
When you come in the room
When you do what only you can do
It changes us, it changes
What we see and what we seek
You're changing everything

Songwriters: Fieldes Mia Leanne Cherie / Sooter Jacob Lee

Spirit of the Living God lyrics © Sony/atv Cross Keys Publishing, Hbc
Worship Music, All Essential Music, Be Essential Songs

Free Draw

This space is for you to illustrate your week, what you are learning, ways God is speaking to you, or maybe draw an image God used to say, "I love YOU."

DAY 4: Step 1- PRAY

Date: _____

Good morning _____,

1. Holy, Holy, Holy are you, Lord God Almighty. You are:

2. Lord, my flesh craves

_____

_____

but I surrender to Your will and Your way. Father, I pray not my will but YOURS be done. Increase my faith to trust you with this.

3. You are the Alpha and Omega. Thank you for going before me and standing behind me. You know all my needs. Lord, you never fail to provide everything I need. Father, here is a need I lay at your feet...

4. God, there is no other god but you. Father forgive me for forgetting this truth in my actions. Forgive me for serving my selfish desires. Lord, here are my sins and my struggles. I acknowledge them before you, please forgive me for...

5. Father, I struggle to forgive others who have caused me great pain. Lord, help me forgive them as you have forgiven me. Bring to my mind someone I need to forgive and then help me to follow through...

6. Heavenly Father, you are a good Father and every test is for my good. Lord, help me trust you during this trial and remember Your faithfulness. Help me as I face

_____

_____

_____ I pray Father, for your faithful strength to help me stand firm in my faith. I pray you remind me that in every storm, you are working all things for my good. I ask for peace that surpasses all my understanding as we walk through this together.

7. Lord, in you alone is where I find my victory with the enemy. Father, I ask for your armor to cover me. And by your Son's name I claim victory and the enemy must flee. I pray in the name of Jesus, Devil you must leave:

Father, thank you for the people I'm blessed to love. Lord, I place

_____

_____

_____

_____in your hands.

Father help me love my neighbors as You love them. Father, please help...

Free space to add any other requests...

Lord before I open Your Word, I ask you to open my eyes to see what YOU want to reveal to me today.

In the precious name of Jesus I pray all these things,

_____.

Step 2: READ

Scripture read today: _____

What does this passage show me about God's character?
God is faithful to His promises. What promise did you read about today?
What numbers did I see in the Scripture? Why was that detail mentioned?
What word or phrases stood out to me and why?
What word/s do I need to look up the meaning?
List the name of the town mentioned in the passage. Later, when you have more time, google that name. Some Biblical town names have a different name today. What do I know about that town? Have these places been mentioned in another passage of Scripture?
What did I glean from this passage that I need to implement in my life? Take a minute to ask the Lord to help you implement these areas in your life.

Step 3: PRAISE

All about Worship: Worship is merely praising the Lord for being God. Giving thanks and glory to the King of kings. On this page either write, sing, or find some way to show the God of all Creation gratitude for who He is to you. Thank Him for your breath, your life, providing everything you need, and for being a good good Father.

Worship Musical Group Albums recommended:

Lauren Daigle— Look up child

Mercy Me– Almost There

Bethel Music– You Make Me Brave, Victory (Live)

I am They– I am They

Passion– Follow you Anywhere

Hillsong Worship

Toby Mac– The Elements

Meredith Andrews– Worth it All

Chris McClarney—Breakthrough (Live)

Danny Gokey– Haven't Seen it Yet

Various Artists– Your Reckless Love

Rend Collective– The Art of Celebration

Mandisa– Overcomer, What If we were Real, Out of the Dark

Shane & Shane

Tauren Wells

Or google Christian Radio and choose your favorite station and listen to a song or two for the next five minutes. If you like to write your praise down, here is a space for you. If you sing a song, write the title of the song in the box to help you remember the joy you found today.

DAY 5: Step 1- PRAY

Date: _____

Good morning _____,

1. Holy, Holy, Holy are you, Lord God Almighty. You are:

2. Lord, my flesh craves

_____

_____

but I surrender to Your will and Your way. Father, I pray not my will but YOURS be done. Increase my faith to trust you with this.

3. You are the Alpha and Omega. Thank you for going before me and standing behind me. You know all my needs. Lord, you never fail to provide everything I need. Father, here is a need I lay at your feet...

4. God, there is no other god but you. Father forgive me for forgetting this truth in my actions. Forgive me for serving my selfish desires. Lord, here are my sins and my struggles. I acknowledge them before you, please forgive me for...

5. Father, I struggle to forgive others who have caused me great pain. Lord, help me forgive them as you have forgiven me. Bring to my mind someone I need to forgive and then help me to follow through...

6. Heavenly Father, you are a good Father and every test is for my good. Lord, help me trust you during this trial and remember Your faithfulness. Help me as I face

_____

_____

_____ I pray Father, for your faithful strength to help me stand firm in my faith. I pray you remind me that in every storm, you are working all things for my good. I ask for peace that surpasses all my understanding as we walk through this together.

7. Lord, in you alone is where I find my victory with the enemy. Father, I ask for your armor to cover me. And by your Son's name I claim victory and the enemy must flee. I pray in the name of Jesus, Devil you must leave:

Father, thank you for the people I'm blessed to love. Lord, I place

_____

_____

_____

_____in your hands.

Father help me love my neighbors as You love them. Father, please help...

Free space to add any other requests...

Lord before I open Your Word, I ask you to open my eyes to see what YOU want to reveal to me today.

In the precious name of Jesus I pray all these things,

_____.

Step 2: READ

Scripture read today: _____

What does this passage show me about God's character?

God is faithful to His promises. What promise did you read about today?

What numbers did I see in the Scripture? Why was that detail mentioned?

What word or phrases stood out to me and why?

What word/s do I need to look up the meaning?

List the name of the town mentioned in the passage. Later, when you have more time, google that name. Some Biblical town names have a different name today. What do I know about that town? Have these places been mentioned in another passage of Scripture?

What did I glean from this passage that I need to implement in my life? Take a minute to ask the Lord to help you implement these areas in your life.

Step 3: PRAISE

All about Worship: Worship is merely praising the Lord for being God. Giving thanks and glory to the King of kings. On this page either write, sing, or find some way to show the God of all Creation gratitude for who He is to you. Thank Him for your breath, your life, providing everything you need, and for being a good good Father.

Worship Musical Group Albums recommended:

Lauren Daigle— Look up child

Mercy Me– Almost There

Bethel Music– You Make Me Brave, Victory (Live)

I am They– I am They

Passion– Follow you Anywhere

Hillsong Worship

Toby Mac– The Elements

Meredith Andrews– Worth it All

Chris McClarney—Breakthrough (Live)

Danny Gokey– Haven't Seen it Yet

Various Artists– Your Reckless Love

Rend Collective– The Art of Celebration

Mandisa– Overcomer, What If we were Real, Out of the Dark

Shane & Shane

Tauren Wells

Or google Christian Radio and choose your favorite station and listen to a song or two for the next five minutes. If you like to write your praise down, here is a space for you. If you sing a song, write the title of the song in the box to help you remember the joy you found today.

DAY 6: Step 1- PRAY

Good morning _____,

1. Holy, Holy, Holy are you, Lord God Almighty. You are:

2. Lord, my flesh craves

_____

_____

but I surrender to Your will and Your way. Father, I pray not my will but YOURS be done. Increase my faith to trust you with this.

3. You are the Alpha and Omega. Thank you for going before me and standing behind me. You know all my needs. Lord, you never fail to provide everything I need. Father, here is a need I lay at your feet...

4. God, there is no other god but you. Father forgive me for forgetting this truth in my actions. Forgive me for serving my selfish desires. Lord, here are my sins and my struggles. I acknowledge them before you, please forgive me for...

5. Father, I struggle to forgive others who have caused me great pain. Lord, help me forgive them as you have forgiven me. Bring to my mind someone I need to forgive and then help me to follow through...

6. Heavenly Father, you are a good Father and every test is for my good. Lord, help me trust you during this trial and remember Your faithfulness. Help me as I face

_____

_____

_____ I pray Father, for your faithful strength to help me stand firm in my faith. I pray you remind me that in every storm, you are working all things for my good. I ask for peace that surpasses all my understanding as we walk through this together.

7. Lord, in you alone is where I find my victory with the enemy. Father, I ask for your armor to cover me. And by your Son's name I claim victory and the enemy must flee. I pray in the name of Jesus, Devil you must leave:

Father, thank you for the people I'm blessed to love. Lord, I place

_____

_____

_____

_____ in your hands.

Father help me love my neighbors as You love them. Father, please help...

Free space to add any other requests...

Lord before I open Your Word, I ask you to open my eyes to see what YOU want to reveal to me today.

In the precious name of Jesus I pray all these things,

_____.

Step 2: READ

Scripture read today: _____

What does this passage show me about God's character?

God is faithful to His promises. What promise did you read about today?

What numbers did I see in the Scripture? Why was that detail mentioned?

What word or phrases stood out to me and why?

What word/s do I need to look up the meaning?

List the name of the town mentioned in the passage. Later, when you have more time, google that name. Some Biblical town names have a different name today. What do I know about that town? Have these places been mentioned in another passage of Scripture?

What did I glean from this passage that I need to implement in my life? Take a minute to ask the Lord to help you implement these areas in your life.

Step 3: PRAISE

All about Worship: Worship is merely praising the Lord for being God. Giving thanks and glory to the King of kings. On this page either write, sing, or find some way to show the God of all Creation gratitude for who He is to you. Thank Him for your breath, your life, providing everything you need, and for being a good good Father.

Worship Musical Group Albums recommended:

Lauren Daigle— Look up child

Mercy Me– Almost There

Bethel Music– You Make Me Brave, Victory (Live)

I am They– I am They

Passion– Follow you Anywhere

Hillsong Worship

Toby Mac– The Elements

Meredith Andrews– Worth it All

Chris McClarney—Breakthrough (Live)

Danny Gokey– Haven't Seen it Yet

Various Artists– Your Reckless Love

Rend Collective– The Art of Celebration

Mandisa– Overcomer, What If we were Real, Out of the Dark

Shane & Shane

Or google Christian Radio and choose your favorite station and listen to a song or two for the next five minutes. If you like to write your praise down, here is a space for you. If you sing a song, write the title of the song in the box to help you remember the joy you found today.

Week Three

You're now midway to completing this study. Was week two better than the first week? Did you overcome those distractions that jockey for your time? Approaching the third week, I noticed my Morning "Dates" with God became crucial to the start of my day. It didn't matter what was planned for this day; God already worked it all out. By giving God my FIRST moments of the day, He helped me stay on task, accomplishing all <u>His</u> goals for the day. Everything fell into place.

God loves this time with you. Keep showing up and opening your heart to hear His voice. He has something special He wants to speak over you this week. So, guard this time with Him. Resist the evil one's schemes to waver your focus.

Ask the Lord to place His armor on you throughout your week. (Ephesians 6:13-18)

In the past couple of weeks, you have prayed the same three prayers. This week we are going to change it up. ***Remember:*** slow and steady as you build into this relationship with the Lord. God desires an intimate relationship with you, but for us to have this kind of connection with God for the next two weeks, we will need to be personal with Him.

Sin separates us from God because He is Holy. Our sin, however, does not separate us from the love of God found through Jesus Christ. But it does drive a wedge between our connections.

Adam and Eve disobeyed the Lord when they ate from the Tree of Good and Evil causing God to evict them from the Garden of Eden. But even though they received a consequence for their action, God never stopped loving them.

> *"and the Lord God clothed Adam and his wife with garments made from skins of animals."*
>
> *-Genesis 3:21(TLB)*

The creating of the garments was the first blood sacrifice for mankind's sin. God covered His children, providing a way for them to still connect with Him.

The love of God never changes, but to remove the divider that hinders our connection with Him, we must confess our disobedience to the Lord. For the next two weeks, you will be encouraged to confess sins. ***Sin is choosing our fleshly desires over God's commands.*** In short, we're ALL disobedient to the LORD. All of mankind has fallen short of the glory of God. *And it is through the blood of Jesus Christ alone we are redeemed.* (Roman 3:23-26) The grace He bestows is sufficient for us. Shield your mind, because the enemy will unearth sins you've already repented from and received forgiveness for. Don't allow him to play that mind game with you.

> *"He has removed our sins as far away from us as the east is from the west."*
>
> *- Psalm 103:12 (TLB)*

In the name of Jesus, you have already been set free. These two weeks are for times you have not repented for either current or previous disobedience.

Sin is like sweat residue left on white tile. Not everyone sees the imprint left from the body that laid there for a minute to cool down after a run. However, with the right light, the glistening residue takes shape revealing the filth that was left behind.

The Holy Spirit is the light that helps us uncover the areas we need to address, and Jesus is the Swiffer that cleans away the residue our sin leaves behind in our lives. Our guilt and shame are removed, which we were never intended to bear.

> *"With the arrival of Jesus, the Messiah, that fateful dilemma is resolved. Those who enter into Christ's being-here-for-us no longer have to live under a continuous, low-lying black cloud. A new power is in operation. The Spirit of life in Christ, like a strong wind, has magnificently cleared the air, freeing you from a fated lifetime of brutal tyranny at the hands of sin and death."*
>
> *-Romans 8:1-2 (MSG)*

Welcome the freedom found in Christ Jesus.

> *"Because of his kindness, you have been saved through trusting Christ. And even trusting is not of yourselves; it too is a gift from God. Salvation is not a reward for the good we have done, so none of us can take any credit for it."*
>
> *-Ephesians 2:8-9 (TLB)*

This week will you allow God to stir up your soil, unearthing places that you need to embrace grace, forgiveness, and restoration. It's in those moments our bond with God strengthens as we go more in depth with Him. His LOVE pours out in abundance seeping into every hole designed for Him to fill.

This week will you put in the time to become real and vulnerable with the Lord during your dates?

 **Step 1: PRAY-** You will notice blocks 1-3 have become shorter, allowing more space for you to write more of your requests. For the next two weeks as you attend your "Date" with the Lord, focus on praying through numbers 4 & 5 of the Seven ways to seek the Lord. Always begin with #1 before moving on to the next section.

1. *Seek and Acknowledge who God is*

2. *Seek God's will*

3. *Seek God's provision*

4. *Seek God's forgiveness*

5. *Seek to forgive others*

6. *Seek God in times of trials*

7. *Seek God to claim victory over the evil one*

Step 2: READ– The challenge for this week is to *read four-five passages of one chapter and answer the questions* labeled Step 2. Again, this is your study. Keep a pace that works best for you. Just don't stop reading. This is your manna for the day.

Step 3: PRAISE– Allow your praises to ascend as His presence descends on you throughout your day. This week will be intense as you allow God to reveal the areas of your life that you have not requested for forgiveness yet. Hold tight to the promises of the Lord.

"These troubles and sufferings of ours are, after all, quite small and won't last very long. Yet this short time of distress will result in God's richest blessing upon us forever and ever! 18 So we do not look at what we can see right now, the troubles all around us, but we look forward to the joys in heaven which we have not yet seen. The troubles will soon be over, but the joys to come will last forever."

- 2 Corinthians 4: 17-18 (TLB)

Play the song on your heart and sing at the top of your lungs.

Keep your answers simple. If you're running out of space to write, then you might want to purchase a cheap spiral notebook. This week is about restoration. Every restoration requires hard work. But after the work is complete, what a beautiful specimen remains.

Whatever you put in is what you will get out of this study. Are you ready to receive your fresh manna from the Lord every day? Let's begin…

DAY 1: Step 1- PRAY

Date: _____

Good morning _____,

1. Holy, Holy, Holy are you, Lord God Almighty. You are:

2. Increase my faith to trust Your will with...

3. Father, here is a need I lay at your feet...

4. God, there is no other god but you. Father forgive me for forgetting this truth in my actions. Forgive me for serving my selfish desires. Lord, here are my sins and my struggles. I acknowledge them before you, please forgive me for...

5. Father, I struggle to forgive others who have caused me great pain. Lord, help me forgive them as you have forgiven me. Bring to my mind someone I need to forgive and then help me to follow through...

6. *Heavenly Father, you are a good Father and every test is for my good. Lord, help me trust you during this trial and remember Your faithfulness. Help me as I face*

_____

_____

_____ *I pray Father, for your faithful strength to help me stand firm in my faith. I pray you remind me that in every storm, you are working all things for my good. I ask for peace that surpasses all my understanding as we walk through this together.*

7. *Lord, in you alone is where I find my victory with the enemy. Father, I ask for your armor to cover me. And by your Son's name I claim victory and the enemy must flee. I pray in the name of Jesus, Devil you must leave:*

Father, thank you for the people I'm blessed to love. Lord, I place

_____

_____

_____

_____*in your hands.*

Father help me love my neighbors as You love them. Father, please help...

Free space to add any other requests...

Lord before I open Your Word, I ask you to open my eyes to see what YOU want to reveal to me today.

In the precious name of Jesus I pray all these things,

_____.

Step 2: READ

Scripture read today: _____

What does this passage show me about God's character?

God is faithful to His promises. What promise did you read about today?

What numbers did I see in the Scripture? Why was that detail mentioned?

What word or phrases stood out to me and why?

What word/s do I need to look up the meaning?

List the name of the town mentioned in the passage. Later, when you have more time, google that name. Some Biblical town names have a different name today. What do I know about that town? Have these places been mentioned in another passage of Scripture?

What did I glean from this passage that I need to implement in my life? Take a minute to ask the Lord to help you implement these areas in your life.

Step 3: PRAISE

All about Worship: Worship is merely praising the Lord for being God. Giving thanks and glory to the King of kings. On this page either write, sing, or find some way to show the God of all Creation gratitude for who He is to you. Thank Him for your breath, your life, providing everything you need, and for being a good good Father.

Worship Musical Group Albums recommended:

Lauren Daigle— Look up child

Mercy Me– Almost There

Bethel Music– You Make Me Brave, Victory (Live)

I am They– I am They

Passion– Follow you Anywhere

Hillsong Worship

Toby Mac– The Elements

Meredith Andrews– Worth it All

Chris McClarney—Breakthrough (Live)

Danny Gokey– Haven't Seen it Yet

Various Artists– Your Reckless Love

Rend Collective– The Art of Celebration

Mandisa– Overcomer, What If we were Real, Out of the Dark

Shane & Shane

Or google Christian Radio and choose your favorite station and listen to a song or two for the next five minutes. If you like to write your praise down, here is a space for you. If you sing a song, write the title of the song in the box to help you remember the joy you found today.

DAY 2: Step 1- PRAY

Date: _____

Good morning _____,

1. Holy, Holy, Holy are you, Lord God Almighty. You are:

2. Increase my faith to trust Your will with...

3. Father, here is a need I lay at your feet...

4. God, there is no other god but you. Father forgive me for forgetting this truth in my actions. Forgive me for serving my selfish desires. Lord, here are my sins and my struggles. I acknowledge them before you, please forgive me for...

5. Father, I struggle to forgive others who have caused me great pain. Lord, help me forgive them as you have forgiven me. Bring to my mind someone I need to forgive and then help me to follow through...

6. *Heavenly Father, you are a good Father and every test is for my good. Lord, help me trust you during this trial and remember Your faithfulness. Help me as I face*

_____

_____

_____ *I pray Father, for your faithful*

strength to help me stand firm in my faith. I pray you remind me that in every storm, you are working all things for my good. I ask for peace that surpasses all my understanding as we walk through this together.

7. *Lord, in you alone is where I find my victory with the enemy. Father, I ask for your armor to cover me. And by your Son's name I claim victory and the enemy must flee. I pray in the name of Jesus, Devil you must leave:*

Father, thank you for the people I'm blessed to love. Lord, I place

_____

_____

_____

_____*in your hands.*

Father help me love my neighbors as You love them. Father, please help...

Free space to add any other requests...

Lord before I open Your Word, I ask you to open my eyes to see what YOU want to reveal to me today.

In the precious name of Jesus I pray all these things,

_____.

Step 2: READ

Scripture read today: _____

What does this passage show me about God's character?

God is faithful to His promises. What promise did you read about today?

What numbers did I see in the Scripture? Why was that detail mentioned?

What word or phrases stood out to me and why?

What word/s do I need to look up the meaning?

List the name of the town mentioned in the passage. Later, when you have more time, google that name. Some Biblical town names have a different name today. What do I know about that town? Have these places been mentioned in another passage of Scripture?

What did I glean from this passage that I need to implement in my life? Take a minute to ask the Lord to help you implement these areas in your life.

Step 3: PRAISE

All about Worship: Worship is merely praising the Lord for being God. Giving thanks and glory to the King of kings. On this page either write, sing, or find some way to show the God of all Creation gratitude for who He is to you. Thank Him for your breath, your life, providing everything you need, and for being a good good Father.

Worship Musical Group Albums recommended:

Lauren Daigle— Look up child

Mercy Me– Almost There

Bethel Music– You Make Me Brave, Victory (Live)

I am They– I am They

Passion– Follow you Anywhere

Hillsong Worship

Toby Mac– The Elements

Meredith Andrews– Worth it All

Chris McClarney—Breakthrough (Live)

Danny Gokey– Haven't Seen it Yet

Various Artists– Your Reckless Love

Rend Collective– The Art of Celebration

Mandisa– Overcomer, What If we were Real, Out of the Dark

Shane & Shane

Tauren Wells

Or google Christian Radio and choose your favorite station and listen to a song or two for the next five minutes. If you like to write your praise down, here is a space for you. If you sing a song, write the title of the song in the box to help you remember the joy you found today.

DAY 3: Step 1- PRAY

Date: _____

Good morning _____,

1. Holy, Holy, Holy are you, Lord God Almighty. You are:

2. Increase my faith to trust Your will with...

3. Father, here is a need I lay at your feet...

4. God, there is no other god but you. Father forgive me for forgetting this truth in my actions. Forgive me for serving my selfish desires. Lord, here are my sins and my struggles. I acknowledge them before you, please forgive me for...

5. Father, I struggle to forgive others who have caused me great pain. Lord, help me forgive them as you have forgiven me. Bring to my mind someone I need to forgive and then help me to follow through...

6. *Heavenly Father, you are a good Father and every test is for my good. Lord, help me trust you during this trial and remember Your faithfulness. Help me as I face*

_____

_____

_____ *I pray Father, for your faithful strength to help me stand firm in my faith. I pray you remind me that in every storm, you are working all things for my good. I ask for peace that surpasses all my understanding as we walk through this together.*

7. *Lord, in you alone is where I find my victory with the enemy. Father, I ask for your armor to cover me. And by your Son's name I claim victory and the enemy must flee. I pray in the name of Jesus, Devil you must leave:*

Father, thank you for the people I'm blessed to love. Lord, I place

_____

_____

_____

_____*in your hands.*

Father help me love my neighbors as You love them. Father, please help...

Free space to add any other requests...

Lord before I open Your Word, I ask you to open my eyes to see what YOU want to reveal to me today.

In the precious name of Jesus I pray all these things,

_____.

Step 2: READ

Scripture read today: _____

What does this passage show me about God's character?

God is faithful to His promises. What promise did you read about today?

What numbers did I see in the Scripture? Why was that detail mentioned?

What word or phrases stood out to me and why?

What word/s do I need to look up the meaning?

List the name of the town mentioned in the passage. Later, when you have more time, google that name. Some Biblical town names have a different name today. What do I know about that town? Have these places been mentioned in another passage of Scripture?

What did I glean from this passage that I need to implement in my life? Take a minute to ask the Lord to help you implement these areas in your life.

Step 3: PRAISE

All about Worship: Worship is merely praising the Lord for being God. Giving thanks and glory to the King of kings. On this page either write, sing, or find some way to show the God of all Creation gratitude for who He is to you. Thank Him for your breath, your life, providing everything you need, and for being a good good Father.

Worship Musical Group Albums recommended:

Lauren Daigle— Look up child

Mercy Me– Almost There

Bethel Music– You Make Me Brave, Victory (Live)

I am They– I am They

Passion– Follow you Anywhere

Hillsong Worship

Toby Mac– The Elements

Meredith Andrews– Worth it All

Chris McClarney—Breakthrough (Live)

Danny Gokey– Haven't Seen it Yet

Various Artists– Your Reckless Love

Rend Collective– The Art of Celebration

Mandisa– Overcomer, What If we were Real, Out of the Dark

Shane & Shane

Tauren Wells

Or google Christian Radio and choose your favorite station and listen to a song or two for the next five minutes. If you like to write your praise down, here is a space for you. If you sing a song, write the title of the song in the box to help you remember the joy you found today.

Reckless Love Lyrics[7]

Before I spoke a word
You were singing over me
You have been so, so
Good to me
Before I took a breath
You breathed your life in me
You have been so, so
Kind to me
Oh, the overwhelming, never-ending, reckless love of God
Oh, it chases me down, fights 'til I'm found, leaves the 99
I couldn't earn it
I don't deserve it
Still you give yourself away
Oh, the overwhelming, never-ending, reckless love of God
When I was your foe
Still your love fought for me
You have been so, so
Good to me
When I felt no worth
You paid it all for me
You have been so, so
Kind to me

Free Draw

This space is for you to illustrate your week, what you are learning, ways God is speaking to you, or maybe draw an image God used to say, "I love YOU."

DAY 4: Step 1- PRAY

Date: _____

Good morning _____,

1. *Holy, Holy, Holy are you, Lord God Almighty. You are:*

2. *Increase my faith to trust Your will with...*

3. *Father, here is a need I lay at your feet...*

4. *God, there is no other god but you. Father forgive me for forgetting this truth in my actions. Forgive me for serving my selfish desires. Lord, here are my sins and my struggles. I acknowledge them before you, please forgive me for...*

5. *Father, I struggle to forgive others who have caused me great pain. Lord, help me forgive them as you have forgiven me. Bring to my mind someone I need to forgive and then help me to follow through...*

6. Heavenly Father, you are a good Father and every test is for my good. Lord, help me trust you during this trial and remember Your faithfulness. Help me as I face

_____

_____

_____ I pray Father, for your faithful strength to help me stand firm in my faith. I pray you remind me that in every storm, you are working all things for my good. I ask for peace that surpasses all my understanding as we walk through this together.

7. Lord, in you alone is where I find my victory with the enemy. Father, I ask for your armor to cover me. And by your Son's name I claim victory and the enemy must flee. I pray in the name of Jesus, Devil you must leave:

Father, thank you for the people I'm blessed to love. Lord, I place

_____

_____

_____

_____in your hands.

Father help me love my neighbors as You love them. Father, please help...

Free space to add any other requests...

Lord before I open Your Word, I ask you to open my eyes to see what YOU want to reveal to me today.

In the precious name of Jesus I pray all these things,

_____.

Step 2: READ

Scripture read today: _____

> **What does this passage show me about God's character?**

> **God is faithful to His promises. What promise did you read about today?**

> **What numbers did I see in the Scripture? Why was that detail mentioned?**

> **What word or phrases stood out to me and why?**

> **What word/s do I need to look up the meaning?**

> **List the name of the town mentioned in the passage. Later, when you have more time, google that name. Some Biblical town names have a different name today. What do I know about that town? Have these places been mentioned in another passage of Scripture?**

> **What did I glean from this passage that I need to implement in my life? Take a minute to ask the Lord to help you implement these areas in your life.**

Step 3: PRAISE

All about Worship: Worship is merely praising the Lord for being God. Giving thanks and glory to the King of kings. On this page either write, sing, or find some way to show the God of all Creation gratitude for who He is to you. Thank Him for your breath, your life, providing everything you need, and for being a good good Father.

Worship Musical Group Albums recommended:

Lauren Daigle— Look up child

Mercy Me– Almost There

Bethel Music– You Make Me Brave, Victory (Live)

I am They– I am They

Passion– Follow you Anywhere

Hillsong Worship

Toby Mac– The Elements

Meredith Andrews– Worth it All

Chris McClarney—Breakthrough (Live)

Danny Gokey– Haven't Seen it Yet

Various Artists– Your Reckless Love

Rend Collective– The Art of Celebration

Mandisa– Overcomer, What If we were Real, Out of the Dark

Shane & Shane

Tauren Wells

Or google Christian Radio and choose your favorite station and listen to a song or two for the next five minutes. If you like to write your praise down, here is a space for you. If you sing a song, write the title of the song in the box to help you remember the joy you found today.

DAY 5: Step 1- PRAY

Date: _____

Good morning _____,

1. Holy, Holy, Holy are you, Lord God Almighty. You are:

2. Increase my faith to trust Your will with...

3. Father, here is a need I lay at your feet...

4. God, there is no other god but you. Father forgive me for forgetting this truth in my actions. Forgive me for serving my selfish desires. Lord, here are my sins and my struggles. I acknowledge them before you, please forgive me for...

5. Father, I struggle to forgive others who have caused me great pain. Lord, help me forgive them as you have forgiven me. Bring to my mind someone I need to forgive and then help me to follow through...

6. Heavenly Father, you are a good Father and every test is for my good. Lord, help me trust you during this trial and remember Your faithfulness. Help me as I face

_____

_____

_____ I pray Father, for your faithful strength to help me stand firm in my faith. I pray you remind me that in every storm, you are working all things for my good. I ask for peace that surpasses all my understanding as we walk through this together.

7. Lord, in you alone is where I find my victory with the enemy. Father, I ask for your armor to cover me. And by your Son's name I claim victory and the enemy must flee. I pray in the name of Jesus, Devil you must leave:

Father, thank you for the people I'm blessed to love. Lord, I place

_____

_____

_____

_____ in your hands.

Father help me love my neighbors as You love them. Father, please help...

Free space to add any other requests...

Lord before I open Your Word, I ask you to open my eyes to see what YOU want to reveal to me today.

In the precious name of Jesus I pray all these things,

_____.

Step 2: READ

Scripture read today: _____

What does this passage show me about God's character?

God is faithful to His promises. What promise did you read about today?

What numbers did I see in the Scripture? Why was that detail mentioned?

What word or phrases stood out to me and why?

What word/s do I need to look up the meaning?

List the name of the town mentioned in the passage. Later, when you have more time, google that name. Some Biblical town names have a different name today. What do I know about that town? Have these places been mentioned in another passage of Scripture?

What did I glean from this passage that I need to implement in my life? Take a minute to ask the Lord to help you implement these areas in your life.

Step 3: PRAISE

All about Worship: Worship is merely praising the Lord for being God. Giving thanks and glory to the King of kings. On this page either write, sing, or find some way to show the God of all Creation gratitude for who He is to you. Thank Him for your breath, your life, providing everything you need, and for being a good good Father.

Worship Musical Group Albums recommended:

Lauren Daigle— Look up child

Mercy Me– Almost There

Bethel Music– You Make Me Brave, Victory (Live)

I am They– I am They

Passion– Follow you Anywhere

Hillsong Worship

Toby Mac– The Elements

Meredith Andrews– Worth it All

Chris McClarney—Breakthrough (Live)

Danny Gokey– Haven't Seen it Yet

Various Artists– Your Reckless Love

Rend Collective– The Art of Celebration

Mandisa– Overcomer, What If we were Real, Out of the Dark

Shane & Shane

Tauren Wells

Or google Christian Radio and choose your favorite station and listen to a song or two for the next five minutes. If you like to write your praise down, here is a space for you. If you sing a song, write the title of the song in the box to help you remember the joy you found today.

DAY 6: Step 1- PRAY

Date: _____

Good morning _____,

1. Holy, Holy, Holy are you, Lord God Almighty. You are:

2. Increase my faith to trust Your will with...

3. Father, here is a need I lay at your feet...

4. God, there is no other god but you. Father forgive me for forgetting this truth in my actions. Forgive me for serving my selfish desires. Lord, here are my sins and my struggles. I acknowledge them before you, please forgive me for...

5. Father, I struggle to forgive others who have caused me great pain. Lord, help me forgive them as you have forgiven me. Bring to my mind someone I need to forgive and then help me to follow through...

6. Heavenly Father, you are a good Father and every test is for my good. Lord, help me trust you during this trial and remember Your faithfulness. Help me as I face

_____

_____

_____ I pray Father, for your faithful strength to help me stand firm in my faith. I pray you remind me that in every storm, you are working all things for my good. I ask for peace that surpasses all my understanding as we walk through this together.

7. Lord, in you alone is where I find my victory with the enemy. Father, I ask for your armor to cover me. And by your Son's name I claim victory and the enemy must flee. I pray in the name of Jesus, Devil you must leave:

Father, thank you for the people I'm blessed to love. Lord, I place

_____

_____

_____

_____in your hands.

Father help me love my neighbors as You love them. Father, please help...

Free space to add any other requests...

Lord before I open Your Word, I ask you to open my eyes to see what YOU want to reveal to me today.

In the precious name of Jesus I pray all these things,

_____.

Step 2: READ

Scripture read today: _____

What does this passage show me about God's character?

God is faithful to His promises. What promise did you read about today?

What numbers did I see in the Scripture? Why was that detail mentioned?

What word or phrases stood out to me and why?

What word/s do I need to look up the meaning?

List the name of the town mentioned in the passage. Later, when you have more time, google that name. Some Biblical town names have a different name today. What do I know about that town? Have these places been mentioned in another passage of Scripture?

What did I glean from this passage that I need to implement in my life? Take a minute to ask the Lord to help you implement these areas in your life.

Step 3: PRAISE

All about Worship: Worship is merely praising the Lord for being God. Giving thanks and glory to the King of kings. On this page either write, sing, or find some way to show the God of all Creation gratitude for who He is to you. Thank Him for your breath, your life, providing everything you need, and for being a good good Father.

Worship Musical Group Albums recommended:

Lauren Daigle— Look up child

Mercy Me– Almost There

Bethel Music– You Make Me Brave, Victory (Live)

I am They– I am They

Passion– Follow you Anywhere

Hillsong Worship

Toby Mac– The Elements

Meredith Andrews– Worth it All

Chris McClarney—Breakthrough (Live)

Danny Gokey– Haven't Seen it Yet

Various Artists– Your Reckless Love

Rend Collective– The Art of Celebration

Mandisa– Overcomer, What If we were Real, Out of the Dark

Shane & Shane

Tauren Wells

Or google Christian Radio and choose your favorite station and listen to a song or two for the next five minutes. If you like to write your praise down, here is a space for you. If you sing a song, write the title of the song in the box to help you remember the joy you found today.

Week Four

You should be so proud of yourself. You have encountered God on 18 official morning "Dates." Only three more weeks to go. I know last week might have been difficult. Confession is hard, and it typically causes grief as we recognize how our actions grieve the Father.

As a child, we may have gotten away with being disobedient towards our parents, but our parents are human, and are limited. God, on the other hand, is LIMITLESS. This means He knows all and sees all. We can't hide our sin from God.

"God means what he says. What he says goes. His powerful Word is sharp as a surgeon's scalpel, cutting through everything, whether doubt or defense, laying us open to listen and obey. Nothing and no one is impervious to God's Word. We can't get away from it—no matter what."

-Hebrews 4:12-13 (MSG)

"That means you must not give sin a vote in the way you conduct your lives. Don't give it the time of day. Don't even run little errands that are connected with that old way of life. Throw yourselves wholeheartedly and full-time—remember, you've been raised from the dead! —into God's way of doing things. Sin can't tell you how to live. After all, you're not living under that old tyranny any longer. You're living in the freedom of God."

-Romans 6:12-14 (MSG)

Preparing your heart for a bond like no other requires complete honesty.

Not only are we to ask for forgiveness, but we are to extend forgiveness to others as well.

For if you forgive other people when they sin against you, your heavenly Father will also forgive you. But if you do not forgive others their sins, your Father will not forgive your sins.

- Matthew 6:14-15(NIV)

This lesson was difficult for me to grasp. For years, I rationalized why it was fair for me to withhold offering forgiveness to someone who has hurt my loved one. My justification sounded like this…

"Lord, why must I do this? Why must I forgive them? The damage from their actions has affected our whole family. Even worse, their lack of involvement challenges my loved one's self-worth. The thief will never admit to their choices or the havoc they have created. Why Lord would you ask me to forgive this person? Their weeds of destruction have touched us ALL."

And the Lord whispers, "So has your bitterness towards this individual."

Tears stream down my face as I repent. I must choose to forgive so my family can live in freedom. I must choose to forgive, so the Father will forgive me. God reminds me that I put His Son on that cross. It was because of my choices he suffered such a significant loss.

> *How can I not forgive someone who harmed my loved one but expect God to forgive me after His Son suffered and died, because of me?*

When we hold grudges or bitterness towards another, we give life to a weed inside our hearts. If this weed is not plucked from the root, the weed will spread, hindering the good seed from bearing fruit. Are there individuals that you have allowed to steal your joy?

Forgiveness is a word we are so grateful to receive, but so hard for us to offer. We know the Lord requires us to forgive, but how do we offer exoneration to someone who has harmed us or the ones we love? Must we make contact and verbally tell them we forgive them? OR can we forgive them without making contact? ***The answer is be obedient to the way God tells YOU to forgive.***

Here are the three ways God may ask us to forgive.

1. ***Write a letter of forgiveness with no intent to send it and/or say a prayer forgiving that individual.*** There are situations contact shouldn't or can't be made, but we still must forgive them in our hearts.

2. ***Make contact expressing you choose to forgive.*** Maybe you write a letter, text message, phone call, or meet face to face. Even if the perpetrators never admit to their wrongdoing, our orders are to forgive. God didn't set limitations for when we should offer forgiveness. He just says FORGIVE. The ripple effect provides us with the blessings of freedom and the forgiveness from the LORD.

3. ***Both:*** we first forgive without any contact. Then as time goes by, God promotes us to engage with that person, inviting us to share the forgiveness we already offered.

Sometimes those individuals bear our name. Forgiving ourselves for the wrong we have committed towards another, or even God, frees us from the guilt and shame we were never meant to experience.

> *"Adam and his wife, both naked, and they felt no shame."*
>
> *-Genesis 2: 25 (NIV)*

Before the fall of man, man never experienced shame or guilt, and they were completely exposed. They had nothing to hide. The intended relationship between God and man was for nothing to separate them. We have the freedom to be vulnerable, allowing us to reveal everything to God. This week offers you a chance to settle unfinished business. Weather you need to ask for forgiveness or extending forgiveness to another, take time to remove those barriers. Indulge in His freedom to expose your true self, developing the relationship we were meant to have with Him from the beginning.

Step 1: PRAY- This week, you will notice blocks 1-3 are blank for you to write your response for those sections. The focus as you attend your "Date" with the Lord, is to pray through numbers 4 & 5 of the *Seven ways to seek the Lord.* Always begin with #1 before moving on to the next section.

1. *Seek and Acknowledge who God is*

2. *Seek God's will*

3. *Seek God's provision*

4. *Seek God's forgiveness*

5. *Seek to forgive others*

6. *Seek God in times of trials*

7. *Seek God to claim victory over the evil one*

Step 2: READ– *The goal this week is to read half of one chapter and answer the questions.* Again, this is your study. Keep a pace that works best for you. If you're not able to read half of the text, then read 4 to 5 verses at a time. Just don't stop reading. This is your manna for the day. It isn't about quantity, but more about the quality of what you're digesting as you read your Love note from God.

Step 3: PRAISE– This week, thank God for the freedom you have been offered as you work through the different phases of forgiveness. Sometime this week, I would love for you to listen to "Forgiveness" by Matthew West. This song helps me remember the importance of forgiveness and voices my prayer.

Keep your answers simple. If you want a more in-depth understanding of the text, use the resources in the back of the book. The design of this study offers you the freedom to decide how deep you want to go.

Remember, whatever you put in is what you will get out of this study. Are you ready to receive your fresh manna from the Lord every day? Let's begin...

DAY 1: Step 1- PRAY

Date: _____

Good morning _____,

1. Holy, Holy, Holy are you, Lord God Almighty. You are:

2. Increase my faith to trust Your will with...

3. Father, here is a need I lay at your feet...

4. God, there is no other god but you. Father forgive me for forgetting this truth in my actions. Forgive me for serving my selfish desires. Lord, here are my sins and my struggles. I acknowledge them before you, please forgive me for...

5. Father, I struggle to forgive others who have caused me great pain. Lord, help me forgive them as you have forgiven me. Bring to my mind someone I need to forgive and then help me to follow through...

6. Heavenly Father, you are a good Father and every test is for my good. Lord, help me trust you during this trial and remember Your faithfulness. Help me as I face

_____

_____

_____ I pray Father, for your faithful strength to help me stand firm in my faith. I pray you remind me that in every storm, you are working all things for my good. I ask for peace that surpasses all my understanding as we walk through this together.

7. Lord, in you alone is where I find my victory with the enemy. Father, I ask for your armor to cover me. And by your Son's name I claim victory and the enemy must flee. I pray in the name of Jesus, Devil you must leave:

Father, thank you for the people I'm blessed to love. Lord, I place

_____

_____

_____ in your hands.

Father help me love my neighbors as You love them. Father, please help...

Free space to add any other requests...

Lord before I open Your Word, I ask you to open my eyes to see what YOU want to reveal to me today.

In the precious name of Jesus I pray all these things,

_____.

Step 2: READ

Scripture read today: _____

What does this passage show me about God's character?
God is faithful to His promises. What promise did you read about today?
What numbers did I see in the Scripture? Why was that detail mentioned?
What word or phrases stood out to me and why?
What word/s do I need to look up the meaning?
List the name of the town mentioned in the passage. Later, when you have more time, google that name. Some Biblical town names have a different name today. What do I know about that town? Have these places been mentioned in another passage of Scripture?
What did I glean from this passage that I need to implement in my life? Take a minute to ask the Lord to help you implement these areas in your life.

Step 3: PRAISE

All about Worship: Worship is merely praising the Lord for being God. Giving thanks and glory to the King of kings. On this page either write, sing, or find some way to show the God of all Creation gratitude for who He is to you. Thank Him for your breath, your life, providing everything you need, and for being a good good Father.

Worship Musical Group Albums recommended:

Lauren Daigle— Look up child

Mercy Me– Almost There

Bethel Music– You Make Me Brave, Victory (Live)

I am They– I am They

Passion– Follow you Anywhere

Hillsong Worship

Toby Mac– The Elements

Meredith Andrews– Worth it All

Chris McClarney—Breakthrough (Live)

Danny Gokey– Haven't Seen it Yet

Various Artists– Your Reckless Love

Rend Collective– The Art of Celebration

Mandisa– Overcomer, What If we were Real, Out of the Dark

Shane & Shane

Tauren Wells

Or google Christian Radio and choose your favorite station and listen to a song or two for the next five minutes. If you like to write your praise down, here is a space for you. If you sing a song, write the title of the song in the box to help you remember the joy you found today.

DAY 2: Step 1- PRAY

Date: _____

Good morning _____,

1. *Holy, Holy, Holy are you, Lord God Almighty. You are:*

2. *Increase my faith to trust Your will with...*

3. *Father, here is a need I lay at your feet...*

4. *God, there is no other god but you. Father forgive me for forgetting this truth in my actions. Forgive me for serving my selfish desires. Lord, here are my sins and my struggles. I acknowledge them before you, please forgive me for...*

5. *Father, I struggle to forgive others who have caused me great pain. Lord, help me forgive them as you have forgiven me. Bring to my mind someone I need to forgive and then help me to follow through...*

6. Heavenly Father, you are a good Father and every test is for my good. Lord, help me trust you during this trial and remember Your faithfulness. Help me as I face

_____

_____

_____ I pray Father, for your faithful strength to help me stand firm in my faith. I pray you remind me that in every storm, you are working all things for my good. I ask for peace that surpasses all my understanding as we walk through this together.

7. Lord, in you alone is where I find my victory with the enemy. Father, I ask for your armor to cover me. And by your Son's name I claim victory and the enemy must flee. I pray in the name of Jesus, Devil you must leave:

Father, thank you for the people I'm blessed to love. Lord, I place

_____

_____

_____in your hands.

Father help me love my neighbors as You love them. Father, please help...

Free space to add any other requests...

Lord before I open Your Word, I ask you to open my eyes to see what YOU want to reveal to me today.

In the precious name of Jesus I pray all these things,

_____.

Step 2: READ

Scripture read today: _____

What does this passage show me about God's character?
God is faithful to His promises. What promise did you read about today?
What numbers did I see in the Scripture? Why was that detail mentioned?
What word or phrases stood out to me and why?
What word/s do I need to look up the meaning?
List the name of the town mentioned in the passage. Later, when you have more time, google that name. Some Biblical town names have a different name today. What do I know about that town? Have these places been mentioned in another passage of Scripture?
What did I glean from this passage that I need to implement in my life? Take a minute to ask the Lord to help you implement these areas in your life.

Step 3: PRAISE

All about Worship: Worship is merely praising the Lord for being God. Giving thanks and glory to the King of kings. This page either write, sing, or find some way to show the God of all Creation gratitude for who He is to you. Thank Him for your breath, your life, providing everything you need, and for being a good good Father.

Worship Musical Group Albums recommended:

Lauren Daigle— Look up child

Mercy Me– Almost There

Bethel Music– You Make Me Brave, Victory (Live)

I am They– I am They

Passion– Follow you Anywhere

Hillsong Worship

Toby Mac– The Elements

Meredith Andrews– Worth it All

Chris McClarney—Breakthrough (Live)

Danny Gokey– Haven't Seen it Yet

Various Artists– Your Reckless Love

Rend Collective– The Art of Celebration

Mandisa– Overcomer, What If we were Real, Out of the Dark

Shane & Shane

Tauren Wells

Or google Christian Radio and choose your favorite station and listen to a song or two for the next five minutes. If you like to write your praise down, here is a space for you. If you sing a song, write the title of the song in the box to help you remember the joy you found today.

DAY 3: Step 1- PRAY

Date: _____

Good morning _____,

> 1. Holy, Holy, Holy are you, Lord God Almighty. You are:

2. Increase my faith to trust Your will with...

3. Father, here is a need I lay at your feet...

4. God, there is no other god but you. Father forgive me for forgetting this truth in my actions. Forgive me for serving my selfish desires. Lord, here are my sins and my struggles. I acknowledge them before you, please forgive me for...

5. Father, I struggle to forgive others who have caused me great pain. Lord, help me forgive them as you have forgiven me. Bring to my mind someone I need to forgive and then help me to follow through...

6. Heavenly Father, you are a good Father and every test is for my good. Lord, help me trust you during this trial and remember Your faithfulness. Help me as I face

_____

_____

_____ I pray Father, for your faithful strength to help me stand firm in my faith. I pray you remind me that in every storm, you are working all things for my good. I ask for peace that surpasses all my understanding as we walk through this together.

7. Lord, in you alone is where I find my victory with the enemy. Father, I ask for your armor to cover me. And by your Son's name I claim victory and the enemy must flee. I pray in the name of Jesus, Devil you must leave:

Father, thank you for the people I'm blessed to love. Lord, I place

_____

_____

_____

_____in your hands.

Father help me love my neighbors as You love them. Father, please help...

Free space to add any other requests...

Lord before I open Your Word, I ask you to open my eyes to see what YOU want to reveal to me today.

In the precious name of Jesus I pray all these things,

_____.

Step 2: READ

Scripture read today: _____

What does this passage show me about God's character?

God is faithful to His promises. What promise did you read about today?

What numbers did I see in the Scripture? Why was that detail mentioned?

What word or phrases stood out to me and why?

What word/s do I need to look up the meaning?

List the name of the town mentioned in the passage. Later, when you have more time, google that name. Some Biblical town names have a different name today. What do I know about that town? Have these places been mentioned in another passage of Scripture?

What did I glean from this passage that I need to implement in my life? Take a minute to ask the Lord to help you implement these areas in your life.

Step 3: PRAISE

All about Worship: Worship is merely praising the Lord for being God. Giving thanks and glory to the King of kings. On this page either write, sing, or find some way to show the God of all Creation gratitude for who He is to you. Thank Him for your breath, your life, providing everything you need, and for being a good good Father.

Worship Musical Group Albums recommended:

Lauren Daigle— Look up child

Mercy Me– Almost There

Bethel Music– You Make Me Brave, Victory (Live)

I am They– I am They

Passion– Follow you Anywhere

Hillsong Worship

Toby Mac– The Elements

Meredith Andrews– Worth it All

Chris McClarney—Breakthrough (Live)

Danny Gokey– Haven't Seen it Yet

Various Artists– Your Reckless Love

Rend Collective– The Art of Celebration

Mandisa– Overcomer, What If we were Real, Out of the Dark

Shane & Shane

Tauren Wells

Or google Christian Radio and choose your favorite station and listen to a song or two for the next five minutes. If you like to write your praise down, here is a space for you. If you sing a song, write the title of the song in the box to help you remember the joy you found today.

Break Every Chain [8]

There is power in the name of Jesus
There is power in the name of Jesus
There is power in the name of Jesus
To break every chain, break every chain
To break every chain
There is power in the name of Jesus
There is power in the name of Jesus
There is power in the name of Jesus
To break every chain, to break every chain
To break every chain
To break every chain, break every chain
Break every chain
And all-sufficient sacrifice, so freely given
Such a price bought our redemption
Heaven's gates swing wide
We believe
There is power in the name of Jesus
There is power in the name of Jesus
There is power in the name of Jesus
To break every chain, break every chain
Break every chain
There is power in the name of Jesus
There is power in the name of Jesus
There is power in the name of Jesus
To break every chain, break every chain
Break every chain
To break every chain, break every chain
Break every chain

Free Draw

This space is for you to illustrate your week, what you are learning, ways God is speaking to you, or maybe draw an image God used to say, "I love YOU."

DAY 4: Step 1- PRAY

Date: _____

Good morning _____,

1. Holy, Holy, Holy are you, Lord God Almighty. You are:

2. Increase my faith to trust Your will with...

3. Father, here is a need I lay at your feet...

4. God, there is no other god but you. Father forgive me for forgetting this truth in my actions. Forgive me for serving my selfish desires. Lord, here are my sins and my struggles. I acknowledge them before you, please forgive me for...

5. Father, I struggle to forgive others who have caused me great pain. Lord, help me forgive them as you have forgiven me. Bring to my mind someone I need to forgive and then help me to follow through...

6. Heavenly Father, you are a good Father and every test is for my good. Lord, help me trust you during this trial and remember Your faithfulness. Help me as I face

_____

_____

_____ I pray Father, for your faithful strength to help me stand firm in my faith. I pray you remind me that in every storm, you are working all things for my good. I ask for peace that surpasses all my understanding as we walk through this together.

7. Lord, in you alone is where I find my victory with the enemy. Father, I ask for your armor to cover me. And by your Son's name I claim victory and the enemy must flee. I pray in the name of Jesus, Devil you must leave:

Father, thank you for the people I'm blessed to love. Lord, I place

_____

_____

_____

_____in your hands.

Father help me love my neighbors as You love them. Father, please help...

Free space to add any other requests...

Lord before I open Your Word, I ask you to open my eyes to see what YOU want to reveal to me today.

In the precious name of Jesus I pray all these things,

_____.

Step 2: READ

Scripture read today: _____

What does this passage show me about God's character?

God is faithful to His promises. What promise did you read about today?

What numbers did I see in the Scripture? Why was that detail mentioned?

What word or phrases stood out to me and why?

What word/s do I need to look up the meaning?

List the name of the town mentioned in the passage. Later, when you have more time, google that name. Some Biblical town names have a different name today. What do I know about that town? Have these places been mentioned in another passage of Scripture?

What did I glean from this passage that I need to implement in my life? Take a minute to ask the Lord to help you implement these areas in your life.

Step 3: PRAISE

All about Worship: Worship is merely praising the Lord for being God. Giving thanks and glory to the King of kings. On this page either write, sing, or find some way to show the God of all Creation gratitude for who He is to you. Thank Him for your breath, your life, providing everything you need, and for being a good good Father.

Worship Musical Group Albums recommended:

Lauren Daigle— Look up child

Mercy Me– Almost There

Bethel Music– You Make Me Brave, Victory (Live)

I am They– I am They

Passion– Follow you Anywhere

Hillsong Worship

Toby Mac– The Elements

Meredith Andrews– Worth it All

Chris McClarney—Breakthrough (Live)

Danny Gokey– Haven't Seen it Yet

Various Artists– Your Reckless Love

Rend Collective– The Art of Celebration

Mandisa– Overcomer, What If we were Real, Out of the Dark

Shane & Shane

Tauren Wells

Or google Christian Radio and choose your favorite station and listen to a song or two for the next five minutes. If you like to write your praise down, here is a space for you. If you sing a song, write the title of the song in the box to help you remember the joy you found today.

DAY 5: Step 1- PRAY

Date: _____

Good morning _____,

1. Holy, Holy, Holy are you, Lord God Almighty. You are:

2. Increase my faith to trust Your will with...

3. Father, here is a need I lay at your feet...

4. God, there is no other god but you. Father forgive me for forgetting this truth in my actions. Forgive me for serving my selfish desires. Lord, here are my sins and my struggles. I acknowledge them before you, please forgive me for...

5. Father, I struggle to forgive others who have caused me great pain. Lord, help me forgive them as you have forgiven me. Bring to my mind someone I need to forgive and then help me to follow through...

6. Heavenly Father, you are a good Father and every test is for my good. Lord, help me trust you during this trial and remember Your faithfulness. Help me as I face

_____

_____

_____ I pray Father, for your faithful strength to help me stand firm in my faith. I pray you remind me that in every storm, you are working all things for my good. I ask for peace that surpasses all my understanding as we walk through this together.

7. Lord, in you alone is where I find my victory with the enemy. Father, I ask for your armor to cover me. And by your Son's name I claim victory and the enemy must flee. I pray in the name of Jesus, Devil you must leave:

Father, thank you for the people I'm blessed to love. Lord, I place

_____

_____

_____

_____in your hands.

Father help me love my neighbors as You love them. Father, please help...

Free space to add any other requests...

Lord before I open Your Word, I ask you to open my eyes to see what YOU want to reveal to me today.

In the precious name of Jesus I pray all these things,

_____.

Step 2: READ

Scripture read today: _____

What does this passage show me about God's character?

God is faithful to His promises. What promise did you read about today?

What numbers did I see in the Scripture? Why was that detail mentioned?

What word or phrases stood out to me and why?

What word/s do I need to look up the meaning?

List the name of the town mentioned in the passage. Later, when you have more time, google that name. Some Biblical town names have a different name today. What do I know about that town? Have these places been mentioned in another passage of Scripture?

What did I glean from this passage that I need to implement in my life? Take a minute to ask the Lord to help you implement these areas in your life.

Step 3: PRAISE

All about Worship: Worship is merely praising the Lord for being God. Giving thanks and glory to the King of kings. On this page either write, sing, or find some way to show the God of all Creation gratitude for who He is to you. Thank Him for your breath, your life, providing everything you need, and for being a good good Father.

Worship Musical Group Albums recommended:

Lauren Daigle— Look up child

Mercy Me– Almost There

Bethel Music– You Make Me Brave, Victory (Live)

I am They– I am They

Passion– Follow you Anywhere

Hillsong Worship

Toby Mac– The Elements

Meredith Andrews– Worth it All

Chris McClarney—Breakthrough (Live)

Danny Gokey– Haven't Seen it Yet

Various Artists– Your Reckless Love

Rend Collective– The Art of Celebration

Mandisa– Overcomer, What If we were Real, Out of the Dark

Shane & Shane

Tauren Wells

Or google Christian Radio and choose your favorite station and listen to a song or two for the next five minutes. If you like to write your praise down, here is a space for you. If you sing a song, write the title of the song in the box to help you remember the joy you found today.

DAY 6: Step 1- PRAY

Date: _____

Good morning _____,

1. Holy, Holy, Holy are you, Lord God Almighty. You are:

2. Increase my faith to trust Your will with...

3. Father, here is a need I lay at your feet...

4. God, there is no other god but you. Father forgive me for forgetting this truth in my actions. Forgive me for serving my selfish desires. Lord, here are my sins and my struggles. I acknowledge them before you, please forgive me for...

5. Father, I struggle to forgive others who have caused me great pain. Lord, help me forgive them as you have forgiven me. Bring to my mind someone I need to forgive and then help me to follow through...

6. Heavenly Father, you are a good Father and every test is for my good. Lord, help me trust you during this trial and remember Your faithfulness. Help me as I face

_____

_____

_____ I pray Father, for your faithful strength to help me stand firm in my faith. I pray you remind me that in every storm, you are working all things for my good. I ask for peace that surpasses all my understanding as we walk through this together.

7. Lord, in you alone is where I find my victory with the enemy. Father, I ask for your armor to cover me. And by your Son's name I claim victory and the enemy must flee. I pray in the name of Jesus, Devil you must leave:

Father, thank you for the people I'm blessed to love. Lord, I place

_____

_____

_____

_____in your hands.

Father help me love my neighbors as You love them. Father, please help...

Free space to add any other requests...

Lord before I open Your Word, I ask you to open my eyes to see what YOU want to reveal to me today.

In the precious name of Jesus I pray all these things,

_____.

Step 2: READ

Scripture read today: _____

What does this passage show me about God's character?

God is faithful to His promises. What promise did you read about today?

What numbers did I see in the Scripture? Why was that detail mentioned?

What word or phrases stood out to me and why?

What word/s do I need to look up the meaning?

List the name of the town mentioned in the passage. Later, when you have more time, google that name. Some Biblical town names have a different name today. What do I know about that town? Have these places been mentioned in another passage of Scripture?

What did I glean from this passage that I need to implement in my life? Take a minute to ask the Lord to help you implement these areas in your life.

Step 3: PRAISE

All about Worship: Worship is merely praising the Lord for being God. Giving thanks and glory to the King of kings. On this page either write, sing, or find some way to show the God of all Creation gratitude for who He is to you. Thank Him for your breath, your life, providing everything you need, and for being a good good Father.

Worship Musical Group Albums recommended:

Lauren Daigle— Look up child

Mercy Me– Almost There

Bethel Music– You Make Me Brave, Victory (Live)

I am They– I am They

Passion– Follow you Anywhere

Hillsong Worship

Toby Mac– The Elements

Meredith Andrews– Worth it All

Chris McClarney—Breakthrough (Live)

Danny Gokey– Haven't Seen it Yet

Various Artists– Your Reckless Love

Rend Collective– The Art of Celebration

Mandisa– Overcomer, What If we were Real, Out of the Dark

Shane & Shane

Tauren Wells

Or google Christian Radio and choose your favorite station and listen to a song or two for the next five minutes. If you like to write your praise down, here is a space for you. If you sing a song, write the title of the song in the box to help you remember the joy you found today.

Week Five

You're doing it! ONLY *two more weeks to go*. I pray you're finding your stride now and anticipating your mornings with the Lover of your soul. This week we'll focus on battling the evil one. You'll need to make sure your armor is on throughout the week. Keep resisting the enemy's attempts to distract you.

Before we begin, the words God spoke over the Israelites before they claimed their promised land are the same words God speaks over you.

> *"Above all, be strong and very courageous to carefully observe the whole instruction My servant Moses commanded you. Do not turn from it to the right or the left, so that you will have success wherever you go. This book of instruction must not depart from your mouth; you are to recite it day and night so that you may carefully observe everything written in it. For then you will prosper and succeed in whatever you do."*
>
> *Joshua 1:7-8 (HCSB)*

When we do battle with the enemy, he will do his best to get us to withdraw. But take courage. The LORD is with you. Our 15 minute "Dates" with the Lord prepare us for battle. Jesus has already won the war.

> *"Because of your little faith," Jesus told them. "For if you had faith even as small as a tiny mustard seed, you could say to this mountain, 'Move!' and it would go far away. Nothing would be impossible. 21 But this kind of demon won't leave unless you have prayed and gone without food."*
>
> *-Matthew 17: 20-21 (TLB)*

There are times when I feel the weight of the world on my shoulders. I recall one of those moments recently. As I watched the descent of the sun announcing the day was over, and tomorrow had yet to begun, water leaked out of the corner of my eye. My request seemed to linger in empty space above my lips as I begged for the waters to part. Temptation lurked, enticing me to give up and stop inquiring God to move this mountain. And then, HE reminded me of His faithfulness. He restored my faith, the size of a mustard seed, to keep pressing onward and walk in faith and not by sight.

When our faith teeters back and forth, weariness creeps in. Desperate requests for instant change weigh heavily on our hearts. Our minds begin to wander and puzzle at our motionless state. In those numb moments, we are reminded... *Faith, the size of a mustard seed, has the power to move our mountain.*

However, repositioning a mountain may take time and be a slow process. Yet, there are other times our mountain is vanquished so abruptly, causing our knees to wobble.

We have no control over a mountain, nor the strength to nudge it. The only one who can relocate a mountain is the ONE who created it. When or how the mountain moves are entirely up to God alone. We are to trust His perfect timing and believe God fulfills every promise.

Speak the victory over your loved ones, your home, your promise, etc. This week build your confidence in the Lord to do what He said He would do. Trust the Lord to fulfill His promises. God is hard at work even when there is no evidence yet that He is working. God is good, and you can count on Him to guide you or your loved one. Sweet friend hold onto His promise.

> *"Consider it a sheer gift, friends, when tests and challenges come at you from all sides. You know that under pressure, your faith-life is forced into the open and shows its true colors. So don't try to get out of anything prematurely. Let it do its work so you become mature and well-developed, not deficient in any way."*
>
> *-James 1:2-4 (MSG)*

Let's evaluate the pace since we bumped it up a notch. Were you able to glean meaning when reading half of the chapter? If not, give yourself grace. There are some extensive chapters in the Bible that can take a couple of days to finish. Moderation is good for our stamina. Don't give up!

Step 1: PRAY- You will notice blocks 4 & 5 have become shorter, allowing more space for you to write more of your requests. For the next two weeks as you attend your "Date" with the Lord, focus on praying through numbers 6 & 7 of the Seven ways to seek the Lord. Always begin with #1 before moving on to the next section.

1. *Seek and Acknowledge who God is*

2. *Seek God's will*

3. *Seek God's provision*

4. *Seek God's forgiveness*

5. *Seek to forgive others*

6. *Seek God in times of trials*

7. *Seek God to claim victory over the evil one*

Step 2: READ- *Read half of one chapter and answer the questions about the chapter in the book of your choice. Keep a pace that works best for you. Just don't stop reading. This is your manna for the day. It isn't about quantity, but more about the quality of what you're digesting from your Love note from God.*

Step 3: PRAISE- play songs glorifying God

"Sing praises to the Lord! Raise your voice in song to him who rides upon the clouds! Jehovah is his name—oh, rejoice in his presence."

-Psalm 68:4 (TLB)

When worry hits you like a freight train causing you great grief, SING. You may not feel like singing in that moment, but there is power in Praise and Worship that heals hearts and removes fears. As we began to sing words about our God, who He is, and what He has done for us, we reposition our gaze on the One who is BIGGER than all our giants, including our true enemy.

*"Do not be anxious about anything but in every situation, by prayer and petition, **with thanksgiving**, present your requests to God. And the peace of God, which transcends all understanding, will guard your hearts and your minds in Christ Jesus."*

-Philippians 4:6-7(NIV)

This week keep your answers simple. If you want a more in-depth understanding of the text, use the resources in the back of the book. The design of this study offers you the freedom to decide how much you would like to absorb.

Remember, whatever you put in is what you will get out of this study. Are you ready to receive your fresh manna from the Lord every day? Let's begin…

DAY 1: Step 1- PRAY

Date: _____

Good morning _____,

1. Holy, Holy, Holy are you, Lord God Almighty. You are:

2. Increase my faith to trust Your will with...

3. Father, here is a need I lay at your feet...

4. God, please forgive me for serving my selfish desires. Lord, here are my sins and my struggles...

5. Father, I struggle to forgive others. Lord, help me forgive them as you have forgiven me.

6. Heavenly Father, you are a good Father and every test is for my good. Lord, help me trust you during this trial and remember Your faithfulness. Help me as I face

_____

_____

_____ I pray Father, for your faithful strength to help me stand firm in my faith. I pray you remind me that in every storm, you are working all things for my good. I ask for peace that surpasses all my understanding as we walk through this together.

7. Lord, in you alone is where I find my victory with the enemy. Father, I ask for your armor to cover me. And by your Son's name I claim victory and the enemy must flee. I pray in the name of Jesus, Devil you must leave:

Father, thank you for the people I'm blessed to love. Lord, I place

_____

_____

_____

_____in your hands.

Father help me love my neighbors as You love them. Father, please help...

Free space to add any other requests...

Lord before I open Your Word, I ask you to open my eyes to see what YOU want to reveal to me today.

In the precious name of Jesus I pray all these things,

_____.

Step 2: READ

Scripture read today: _____

What does this passage show me about God's character?

God is faithful to His promises. What promise did you read about today?

What numbers did I see in the Scripture? Why was that detail mentioned?

What word or phrases stood out to me and why?

What word/s do I need to look up the meaning?

List the name of the town mentioned in the passage. Later, when you have more time, google that name. Some Biblical town names have a different name today. What do I know about that town? Have these places been mentioned in another passage of Scripture?

What did I glean from this passage that I need to implement in my life? Take a minute to ask the Lord to help you implement these areas in your life.

Step 3: PRAISE

All about Worship: Worship is merely praising the Lord for being God. Giving thanks and glory to the King of kings. On this page either write, sing, or find some way to show the God of all Creation gratitude for who He is to you. Thank Him for your breath, your life, providing everything you need, and for being a good good Father.

Worship Musical Group Albums recommended:

Lauren Daigle— Look up child

Mercy Me– Almost There

Bethel Music– You Make Me Brave, Victory (Live)

I am They– I am They

Passion– Follow you Anywhere

Hillsong Worship

Toby Mac– The Elements

Meredith Andrews– Worth it All

Chris McClarney—Breakthrough (Live)

Danny Gokey– Haven't Seen it Yet

Various Artists– Your Reckless Love

Rend Collective– The Art of Celebration

Mandisa– Overcomer, What If we were Real, Out of the Dark

Shane & Shane

Tauren Wells

Or google Christian Radio and choose your favorite station and listen to a song or two for the next five minutes. If you like to write your praise down, here is a space for you. If you sing a song, write the title of the song in the box to help you remember the joy you found today.

DAY 2: Step 1- PRAY

Good morning _____,

1. Holy, Holy, Holy are you, Lord God Almighty. You are:

2. Increase my faith to trust Your will with...

3. Father, here is a need I lay at your feet...

4. God, please forgive me for serving my selfish desires. Lord, here are my sins and my struggles...

5. Father, I struggle to forgive others. Lord, help me forgive them as you have forgiven me.

6. Heavenly Father, you are a good Father and every test is for my good. Lord, help me trust you during this trial and remember Your faithfulness. Help me as I face

_____

_____

_____ I pray Father, for your faithful strength to help me stand firm in my faith. I pray you remind me that in every storm, you are working all things for my good. I ask for peace that surpasses all my understanding as we walk through this together.

7. Lord, in you alone is where I find my victory with the enemy. Father, I ask for your armor to cover me. And by your Son's name I claim victory and the enemy must flee. I pray in the name of Jesus, Devil you must leave:

Father, thank you for the people I'm blessed to love. Lord, I place

_____

_____

_____ in your hands.

Father help me love my neighbors as You love them. Father, please help...

Free space to add any other requests...

Lord before I open Your Word, I ask you to open my eyes to see what YOU want to reveal to me today.

In the precious name of Jesus I pray all these things,

_____.

Step 2: READ

Scripture read today: _____

> **What does this passage show me about God's character?**

> **God is faithful to His promises. What promise did you read about today?**

> **What numbers did I see in the Scripture? Why was that detail mentioned?**

> **What word or phrases stood out to me and why?**

> **What word/s do I need to look up the meaning?**

> **List the name of the town mentioned in the passage. Later, when you have more time, google that name. Some Biblical town names have a different name today. What do I know about that town? Have these places been mentioned in another passage of Scripture?**

> **What did I glean from this passage that I need to implement in my life? Take a minute to ask the Lord to help you implement these areas in your life.**

Step 3: PRAISE

All about Worship: Worship is merely praising the Lord for being God. Giving thanks and glory to the King of kings. On this page either write, sing, or find some way to show the God of all Creation gratitude for who He is to you. Thank Him for your breath, your life, providing everything you need, and for being a good good Father.

Worship Musical Group Albums recommended:

Lauren Daigle— Look up child

Mercy Me– Almost There

Bethel Music– You Make Me Brave, Victory (Live)

I am They– I am They

Passion– Follow you Anywhere

Hillsong Worship

Toby Mac– The Elements

Meredith Andrews– Worth it All

Chris McClarney—Breakthrough (Live)

Danny Gokey– Haven't Seen it Yet

Various Artists– Your Reckless Love

Rend Collective– The Art of Celebration

Mandisa– Overcomer, What If we were Real, Out of the Dark

Shane & Shane

Tauren Wells

Or google Christian Radio and choose your favorite station and listen to a song or two for the next five minutes. If you like to write your praise down, here is a space for you. If you sing a song, write the title of the song in the box to help you remember the joy you found today.

DAY 3: Step 1- PRAY

Date: _____

Good morning _____,

1. Holy, Holy, Holy are you, Lord God Almighty. You are:

2. Increase my faith to trust Your will with...

3. Father, here is a need I lay at your feet...

4. God, please forgive me for serving my selfish desires. Lord, here are my sins and my struggles...

5. Father, I struggle to forgive others. Lord, help me forgive them as you have forgiven me.

6. Heavenly Father, you are a good Father and every test is for my good. Lord, help me trust you during this trial and remember Your faithfulness. Help me as I face

_____

_____

_____ I pray Father, for your faithful strength to help me stand firm in my faith. I pray you remind me that in every storm, you are working all things for my good. I ask for peace that surpasses all my understanding as we walk through this together.

7. Lord, in you alone is where I find my victory with the enemy. Father, I ask for your armor to cover me. And by your Son's name I claim victory and the enemy must flee. I pray in the name of Jesus, Devil you must leave:

Father, thank you for the people I'm blessed to love. Lord, I place

_____

_____

_____

_____in your hands.

Father help me love my neighbors as You love them. Father, please help...

Free space to add any other requests...

Lord before I open Your Word, I ask you to open my eyes to see what YOU want to reveal to me today.

In the precious name of Jesus I pray all these things,

_____.

Step 2: READ

Scripture read today: _____

What does this passage show me about God's character?

God is faithful to His promises. What promise did you read about today?

What numbers did I see in the Scripture? Why was that detail mentioned?

What word or phrases stood out to me and why?

What word/s do I need to look up the meaning?

List the name of the town mentioned in the passage. Later, when you have more time, google that name. Some Biblical town names have a different name today. What do I know about that town? Have these places been mentioned in another passage of Scripture?

What did I glean from this passage that I need to implement in my life? Take a minute to ask the Lord to help you implement these areas in your life.

Step 3: PRAISE

All about Worship: Worship is merely praising the Lord for being God. Giving thanks and glory to the King of kings. On this page either write, sing, or find some way to show the God of all Creation gratitude for who He is to you. Thank Him for your breath, your life, providing everything you need, and for being a good good Father.

Worship Musical Group Albums recommended:

Lauren Daigle— Look up child

Mercy Me– Almost There

Bethel Music– You Make Me Brave, Victory (Live)

I am They– I am They

Passion– Follow you Anywhere

Hillsong Worship

Toby Mac– The Elements

Meredith Andrews– Worth it All

Chris McClarney—Breakthrough (Live)

Danny Gokey– Haven't Seen it Yet

Various Artists– Your Reckless Love

Rend Collective– The Art of Celebration

Mandisa– Overcomer, What If we were Real, Out of the Dark

Shane & Shane

Tauren Wells

> *Or google Christian Radio and choose your favorite station and listen to a song or two for the next five minutes. If you like to write your praise down, here is a space for you. If you sing a song, write the title of the song in the box to help you remember the joy you found today.*

Give Me Faith[9]

I need you to soften my heart
And break me apart
I need you to open my eyes
To see that You're shaping my life

All I am, I surrender

Give me faith to trust what you say
That you're good and your love is great
I'm broken inside, I give you my life

All I am, I surrender

I need you to soften my heart
And break me apart
I need you to pierce through the dark
And cleanse every part of me

'Cause I may be weak
But Your spirit strong in me
My flesh may fail
My God you never will
I may be weak
But Your spirit strong in me
My flesh may fail
My God you never will

Give me faith to trust what you say
That you're good and your love is great
I'm broken inside, I give you my life

Songwriters: Christopher Joel Brown / London Weidberg Gatch / Mack Donald Iii Brock /
Wade Joye
Give Me Faith lyrics © Essential Music Publishing

Free Draw

This space is for you to illustrate your week, what you are learning, ways God is speaking to you, or maybe draw an image God used to say, "I love YOU."

DAY 4: Step 1- PRAY

Date: _____

Good morning _____,

1. Holy, Holy, Holy are you, Lord God Almighty. You are:

2. Increase my faith to trust Your will with...

3. Father, here is a need I lay at your feet...

4. God, please forgive me for serving my selfish desires. Lord, here are my sins and my struggles...

5. Father, I struggle to forgive others. Lord, help me forgive them as you have forgiven me.

6. Heavenly Father, you are a good Father and every test is for my good. Lord, help me trust you during this trial and remember Your faithfulness. Help me as I face

_____

_____

_____ I pray Father, for your faithful strength to help me stand firm in my faith. I pray you remind me that in every storm, you are working all things for my good. I ask for peace that surpasses all my understanding as we walk through this together.

7. Lord, in you alone is where I find my victory with the enemy. Father, I ask for your armor to cover me. And by your Son's name I claim victory and the enemy must flee. I pray in the name of Jesus, Devil you must leave:

Father, thank you for the people I'm blessed to love. Lord, I place

_____

_____

_____

_____in your hands.

Father help me love my neighbors as You love them. Father, please help...

Free space to add any other requests...

Lord before I open Your Word, I ask you to open my eyes to see what YOU want to reveal to me today.

In the precious name of Jesus I pray all these things,

_____.

Step 2: READ

Scripture read today: _____

What does this passage show me about God's character?

God is faithful to His promises. What promise did you read about today?

What numbers did I see in the Scripture? Why was that detail mentioned?

What word or phrases stood out to me and why?

What word/s do I need to look up the meaning?

List the name of the town mentioned in the passage. Later, when you have more time, google that name. Some Biblical town names have a different name today. What do I know about that town? Have these places been mentioned in another passage of Scripture?

What did I glean from this passage that I need to implement in my life? Take a minute to ask the Lord to help you implement these areas in your life.

Step 3: PRAISE

All about Worship: Worship is merely praising the Lord for being God. Giving thanks and glory to the King of kings. On this page either write, sing, or find some way to show the God of all Creation gratitude for who He is to you. Thank Him for your breath, your life, providing everything you need, and for being a good good Father.

Worship Musical Group Albums recommended:

Lauren Daigle— Look up child

Mercy Me– Almost There

Bethel Music– You Make Me Brave, Victory (Live)

I am They– I am They

Passion– Follow you Anywhere

Hillsong Worship

Toby Mac– The Elements

Meredith Andrews– Worth it All

Chris McClarney—Breakthrough (Live)

Danny Gokey– Haven't Seen it Yet

Various Artists– Your Reckless Love

Rend Collective– The Art of Celebration

Mandisa– Overcomer, What If we were Real, Out of the Dark

Shane & Shane

Tauren Wells

Or google Christian Radio and choose your favorite station and listen to a song or two for the next five minutes. If you like to write your praise down, here is a space for you. If you sing a song, write the title of the song in the box to help you remember the joy you found today.

DAY 5: Step 1- PRAY

Date: _____

Good morning _____,

1. Holy, Holy, Holy are you, Lord God Almighty. You are:

2. Increase my faith to trust Your will with...

3. Father, here is a need I lay at your feet...

4. God, please forgive me for serving my selfish desires. Lord, here are my sins and my struggles...

5. Father, I struggle to forgive others. Lord, help me forgive them as you have forgiven me.

6. Heavenly Father, you are a good Father and every test is for my good. Lord, help me trust you during this trial and remember Your faithfulness. Help me as I face

_____

_____

_____ I pray Father, for your faithful strength to help me stand firm in my faith. I pray you remind me that in every storm, you are working all things for my good. I ask for peace that surpasses all my understanding as we walk through this together.

7. Lord, in you alone is where I find my victory with the enemy. Father, I ask for your armor to cover me. And by your Son's name I claim victory and the enemy must flee. I pray in the name of Jesus, Devil you must leave:

Father, thank you for the people I'm blessed to love. Lord, I place

_____

_____

_____

_____ in your hands.

Father help me love my neighbors as You love them. Father, please help...

Free space to add any other requests...

Lord before I open Your Word, I ask you to open my eyes to see what YOU want to reveal to me today.

In the precious name of Jesus I pray all these things,

_____.

Step 2: READ

Scripture read today: _____

What does this passage show me about God's character?

God is faithful to His promises. What promise did you read about today?

What numbers did I see in the Scripture? Why was that detail mentioned?

What word or phrases stood out to me and why?

What word/s do I need to look up the meaning?

List the name of the town mentioned in the passage. Later, when you have more time, google that name. Some Biblical town names have a different name today. What do I know about that town? Have these places been mentioned in another passage of Scripture?

What did I glean from this passage that I need to implement in my life? Take a minute to ask the Lord to help you implement these areas in your life.

Step 3: PRAISE

All about Worship: Worship is merely praising the Lord for being God. Giving thanks and glory to the King of kings. On this page either write, sing, or find some way to show the God of all Creation gratitude for who He is to you. Thank Him for your breath, your life, providing everything you need, and for being a good good Father.

Worship Musical Group Albums recommended:

Lauren Daigle— Look up child

Mercy Me– Almost There

Bethel Music– You Make Me Brave, Victory (Live)

I am They– I am They

Passion– Follow you Anywhere

Hillsong Worship

Toby Mac– The Elements

Meredith Andrews– Worth it All

Chris McClarney—Breakthrough (Live)

Danny Gokey– Haven't Seen it Yet

Various Artists– Your Reckless Love

Rend Collective– The Art of Celebration

Mandisa– Overcomer, What If we were Real, Out of the Dark

Shane & Shane

Tauren Wells

Or google Christian Radio and choose your favorite station and listen to a song or two for the next five minutes. If you like to write your praise down, here is a space for you. If you sing a song, write the title of the song in the box to help you remember the joy you found today.

DAY 6: Step 1- PRAY

Date: _____

Good morning _____,

1. Holy, Holy, Holy are you, Lord God Almighty. You are:

2. Increase my faith to trust Your will with...

3. Father, here is a need I lay at your feet...

4. God, please forgive me for serving my selfish desires. Lord, here are my sins and my struggles...

5. Father, I struggle to forgive others. Lord, help me forgive them as you have forgiven me.

6. Heavenly Father, you are a good Father and every test is for my good. Lord, help me trust you during this trial and remember Your faithfulness. Help me as I face

_____

_____

_____ I pray Father, for your faithful strength to help me stand firm in my faith. I pray you remind me that in every storm, you are working all things for my good. I ask for peace that surpasses all my understanding as we walk through this together.

7. Lord, in you alone is where I find my victory with the enemy. Father, I ask for your armor to cover me. And by your Son's name I claim victory and the enemy must flee. I pray in the name of Jesus, Devil you must leave:

Father, thank you for the people I'm blessed to love. Lord, I place

_____

_____

_____

_____ in your hands.

Father help me love my neighbors as You love them. Father, please help...

Free space to add any other requests...

Lord before I open Your Word, I ask you to open my eyes to see what YOU want to reveal to me today.

In the precious name of Jesus I pray all these things,

_____.

Step 2: READ

Scripture read today: _____

What does this passage show me about God's character?

God is faithful to His promises. What promise did you read about today?

What numbers did I see in the Scripture? Why was that detail mentioned?

What word or phrases stood out to me and why?

What word/s do I need to look up the meaning?

List the name of the town mentioned in the passage. Later, when you have more time, google that name. Some Biblical town names have a different name today. What do I know about that town? Have these places been mentioned in another passage of Scripture?

What did I glean from this passage that I need to implement in my life? Take a minute to ask the Lord to help you implement these areas in your life.

Step 3: PRAISE

All about Worship: Worship is merely praising the Lord for being God. Giving thanks and glory to the King of kings. On this page either write, sing, or find some way to show the God of all Creation gratitude for who He is to you. Thank Him for your breath, your life, providing everything you need, and for being a good good Father.

Worship Musical Group Albums recommended:

Lauren Daigle— Look up child

Mercy Me– Almost There

Bethel Music– You Make Me Brave, Victory (Live)

I am They– I am They

Passion– Follow you Anywhere

Hillsong Worship

Toby Mac– The Elements

Meredith Andrews– Worth it All

Chris McClarney—Breakthrough (Live)

Danny Gokey– Haven't Seen it Yet

Various Artists– Your Reckless Love

Rend Collective– The Art of Celebration

Mandisa– Overcomer, What If we were Real, Out of the Dark

Shane & Shane

Tauren Wells

Or google Christian Radio and choose your favorite station and listen to a song or two for the next five minutes. If you like to write your praise down, here is a space for you. If you sing a song, write the title of the song in the box to help you remember the joy you found today.

Week Six

THE LAST WEEK!!!! This week we are going to finish strong. At the end of this week, you will have gone on 40 dates with the Lord. That's a lot of morning "dates." These 40 Days have been so intimate and personal. God loves meeting with you daily.

The number 40 had a purpose, and it wasn't by chance 40 was chosen. There is a reason for all numbers mentioned throughout Scripture, and here is why our study is 6 Weeks/40 Days long.

> *The Israelites had moved about in the wilderness forty years until all the men who were of military age when they left Egypt had died since they had not obeyed the LORD. For the LORD had sworn to them, they would not see the land he solemnly promised their ancestors to give us, a land flowing with milk and honey.*
>
> *-Joshua 5:6 (NIV)*

There is a promised land designed by God for all of us. However, for us to ever see this land flowing with milk and honey, we must let our old selves die. I believe 40 intentional dates with the Lord is how God removes our doubts.

> *"but those who trust in the Lord*
> *will renew their strength;*
> *they will soar on wings like eagles;*
> *they will run and not grow weary;*
> *they will walk and not faint."*
>
> *-Isaiah 40:31 (HCSB)*

Running on the treadmill of life might seem redundant, and the feeling of never getting anywhere can cause us to doubt. Have the unsuspected roadblocks detoured you from following through in your ambition? The verse above reminds me of a keyword I loathe, but desperately need to grasp: *"wait."* Waiting is not something I do well. I rationalize my eagerness for the need to be efficient.

However, waiting on the Lord doesn't mean *"do nothing."* We are to prepare the field, plant the seeds, water the ground, and then wait for God to grow and multiply. This takes work and endurance on our part. Faith is trusting the Lord to produce fruit from the labor He has called us to do.

God bestows gifts on us to fulfill His purpose, but it may take time to see the fruit. A seed doesn't change overnight. Be patient and keep pressing on. This verse also reminds us that while we wait on the LORD, our strength will be renewed.

God never fails to lift the weight of defeat off my shoulders by sending me an encouraging message from a friend or a stranger. But the best affirmation comes in the mornings when I rise with a song in my heart. I open His Word; God speaks directly, validating His plans for me, healing my broken heart. Those are the moments God renews my strength to press on.

Look for those moments when you grow weary. Resist the temptation to derail your path. If it is the will of God, He will sustain you to press on. This work is not for the faint of heart. Hold tight to the hands of the Father as you travel this road. *And when you think of giving up, the breath of God will help you glide, resting your wings as you soar across the sky.*

My prayer and hope is that your minds will be renewed, your hearts begin beating strongly for the Lord, and you have become in tune with God's will for your life. Let's finish strong!

Again, ask the Lord to place His armor on you throughout your week. Keep resisting the enemy's attempts to distract you. Have you been able to keep up the pace since we bumped it up a notch? If you struggled to read half of the chapters last week, give yourself grace. There are some extensive chapters in the Bible that can take a couple of days to finish. Don't give up! Remember, it's not about the number of verses you read. It's more about the quality of what you digest.

Step 1: PRAY– You will notice blocks 6 & 7 have become shorter, allowing more space for you to write more of your requests. For the next week, as you attend your "Date" with the Lord, focus on praying through all of the Seven ways to seek the Lord.

1. *Seek and Acknowledge who God is*

2. *Seek God's will*

3. *Seek God's provision*

4. *Seek God's forgiveness*

5. *Seek to forgive others*

6. *Seek God in times of trials*

7. *Seek God to claim victory over the evil one*

Step 2: READ- *Read one whole chapter a day and answer questions after reading each* of the chapters in the book of your choice. If reading an entire chapter is difficult, I still prefer you to absorb what God wants to show you at your own pace. Whatever works best for you, stick with it. Just don't stop reading. This is your manna for the day. By reading His Word, you are placing God's armor on before you start your day.

Step 3: PRAISE- Another way for us to worship or praise God is to use our abilities. He gives us gifts in order to point others back to Him. These past six weeks, you have spent priceless time with your Creator. When He crafted you in your mother's womb, there was purpose with every detail in your formation. God gifted you with specific talents to use for His glory and they include fruits of the Spirit:

"But when the Holy Spirit controls our lives he will produce this kind of fruit in us: love, joy, peace, patience, kindness, goodness, faithfulness, gentleness and self-control; and here there is no conflict with Jewish laws."
                                                        -Galatians 5:22-23 (TLB)

So, for this week, seek ways to show these gifts toward others as your act of praise to God. Be open to God's prompting as He guides you. Keep your response simple. Remember, if you want a deeper comprehension to help you understand what you're reading today, resources are in the back of the book that have helped me. The design of this study offers you the freedom to decide how deep you want to go.

Remember, whatever you put in is what you will get out of this study. Are you ready to receive your fresh manna from the Lord every day?

Let's begin…

DAY 1: Step 1- PRAY

Date: _____

Good morning _____,

1.

2.

3.

4.

5.

6.

7.

Father, thank you for the people I'm blessed to love. Lord, I place

_____

_____

_____

_____in your hands.

Father help me love my neighbors as You love them. Father, please help...

Free space to add any other requests...

Lord before I open Your Word, I ask you to open my eyes to see what YOU want to reveal to me today.

In the precious name of Jesus I pray all these things,

_____.

Step 2: READ

Scripture read today: _____

What does this passage show me about God's character?

God is faithful to His promises. What promise did you read about today?

What numbers did I see in the Scripture? Why was that detail mentioned?

What word or phrases stood out to me and why?

What word/s do I need to look up the meaning?

List the name of the town mentioned in the passage. Later, when you have more time, google that name. Some Biblical town names have a different name today. What do I know about that town? Have these places been mentioned in another passage of Scripture?

What did I glean from this passage that I need to implement in my life? Take a minute to ask the Lord to help you implement these areas in your life.

Step 3: PRAISE

All about Worship: Worship is merely praising the Lord for being God. Giving thanks and glory to the King of kings. On this page either write, sing, or find some way to show the God of all Creation gratitude for who He is to you. Thank Him for your breath, your life, providing everything you need, and for being a good good Father.

Worship Musical Group Albums recommended:

Lauren Daigle— Look up child

Mercy Me– Almost There

Bethel Music– You Make Me Brave, Victory (Live)

I am They– I am They

Passion– Follow you Anywhere

Hillsong Worship

Toby Mac– The Elements

Meredith Andrews– Worth it All

Chris McClarney—Breakthrough (Live)

Danny Gokey– Haven't Seen it Yet

Various Artists– Your Reckless Love

Rend Collective– The Art of Celebration

Mandisa– Overcomer, What If we were Real, Out of the Dark

Shane & Shane

Tauren Wells

Or google Christian Radio and choose your favorite station and listen to a song or two for the next five minutes. If you like to write your praise down, here is a space for you. If you sing a song, write the title of the song in the box to help you remember the joy you found today.

DAY 2: Step 1- PRAY

Date: _____

Good morning _____,

1.

2.

3.

4.

5.

6.

7.

Father, thank you for the people I'm blessed to love. Lord, I place

_____

_____

_____

_____in your hands.

Father help me love my neighbors as You love them. Father, please help...

Free space to add any other requests...

Lord before I open Your Word, I ask you to open my eyes to see what YOU want to reveal to me today.

In the precious name of Jesus I pray all these things,

_____.

Step 2: READ

Scripture read today: _____

What does this passage show me about God's character?

God is faithful to His promises. What promise did you read about today?

What numbers did I see in the Scripture? Why was that detail mentioned?

What word or phrases stood out to me and why?

What word/s do I need to look up the meaning?

List the name of the town mentioned in the passage. Later, when you have more time, google that name. Some Biblical town names have a different name today. What do I know about that town? Have these places been mentioned in another passage of Scripture?

What did I glean from this passage that I need to implement in my life? Take a minute to ask the Lord to help you implement these areas in your life.

Step 3: PRAISE

All about Worship: Worship is merely praising the Lord for being God. Giving thanks and glory to the King of kings. On this page either write, sing, or find some way to show the God of all Creation gratitude for who He is to you. Thank Him for your breath, your life, providing everything you need, and for being a good good Father.

Worship Musical Group Albums recommended:

Lauren Daigle— Look up child

Mercy Me– Almost There

Bethel Music– You Make Me Brave, Victory (Live)

I am They– I am They

Passion– Follow you Anywhere

Hillsong Worship

Toby Mac– The Elements

Meredith Andrews– Worth it All

Chris McClarney—Breakthrough (Live)

Danny Gokey– Haven't Seen it Yet

Various Artists– Your Reckless Love

Rend Collective– The Art of Celebration

Mandisa– Overcomer, What If we were Real, Out of the Dark

Shane & Shane

Tauren Wells

Or google Christian Radio and choose your favorite station and listen to a song or two for the next five minutes. If you like to write your praise down, here is a space for you. If you sing a song, write the title of the song in the box to help you remember the joy you found today.

DAY 3: Step 1- PRAY

Date: _____

Good morning _____,

1.

2.

3.

4.

5.

6.

7.

Father, thank you for the people I'm blessed to love. Lord, I place

_____

_____

_____

_____in your hands.

Father help me love my neighbors as You love them. Father, please help...

Free space to add any other requests...

Lord before I open Your Word, I ask you to open my eyes to see what YOU want to reveal to me today.

In the precious name of Jesus I pray all these things,

_____.

Step 2: READ

Scripture read today: _____

What does this passage show me about God's character?

God is faithful to His promises. What promise did you read about today?

What numbers did I see in the Scripture? Why was that detail mentioned?

What word or phrases stood out to me and why?

What word/s do I need to look up the meaning?

List the name of the town mentioned in the passage. Later, when you have more time, google that name. Some Biblical town names have a different name today. What do I know about that town? Have these places been mentioned in another passage of Scripture?

What did I glean from this passage that I need to implement in my life? Take a minute to ask the Lord to help you implement these areas in your life.

Step 3: PRAISE

All about Worship: Worship is merely praising the Lord for being God. Giving thanks and glory to the King of kings. On this page either write, sing, or find some way to show the God of all Creation gratitude for who He is to you. Thank Him for your breath, your life, providing everything you need, and for being a good good Father.

Worship Musical Group Albums recommended:

Lauren Daigle— Look up child

Mercy Me– Almost There

Bethel Music– You Make Me Brave, Victory (Live)

I am They– I am They

Passion– Follow you Anywhere

Hillsong Worship

Toby Mac– The Elements

Meredith Andrews– Worth it All

Chris McClarney—Breakthrough (Live)

Danny Gokey– Haven't Seen it Yet

Various Artists– Your Reckless Love

Rend Collective– The Art of Celebration

Mandisa– Overcomer, What If we were Real, Out of the Dark

Shane & Shane

Tauren Wells

Or google Christian Radio and choose your favorite station and listen to a song or two for the next five minutes. If you like to write your praise down, here is a space for you. If you sing a song, write the title of the song in the box to help you remember the joy you found today.

I'm Listening [10]

When You speak, confusion fades

Just a word and suddenly I'm not afraid

'Cause You speak and freedom reigns

There is hope in every single word You say

I don't wanna miss one word You speak

'Cause everything You say is life to me

I don't wanna miss one word You speak

Quiet my heart, I'm listening

When sorrows roar and troubles rage

You whisper peace when I don't have the words to say

I won't lose hope when storms won't break

You keep Your word, oh and Your promises will keep me
safe

I don't wanna miss one word You speak

'Cause everything You say is life to me

I don't wanna miss one word You speak

So quiet my heart, I'm listening

Your ways are higher

You know just what I need

I trust You, Jesus

You see what I cannot see

I don't wanna miss one word You speak

'Cause everything You say is life to me

I don't wanna miss one word You speak

So quiet my heart, I'm listening

Free Draw
This space is for you to illustrate your week, what you are learning, ways God is speaking to you, or maybe draw an image God used to say, "I love YOU."

DAY 4: Step 1- PRAY

Date: _____

Good morning _____,

1.

2.

3.

4.

5.

6.

7.

Father, thank you for the people I'm blessed to love. Lord, I place

_____

_____

_____

_____in your hands.

Father help me love my neighbors as You love them. Father, please help...

Free space to add any other requests...

Lord before I open Your Word, I ask you to open my eyes to see what YOU want to reveal to me today.

In the precious name of Jesus I pray all these things,

_____.

Step 2: READ

Scripture read today: _____

> **What does this passage show me about God's character?**

> **God is faithful to His promises. What promise did you read about today?**

> **What numbers did I see in the Scripture? Why was that detail mentioned?**

> **What word or phrases stood out to me and why?**

> **What word/s do I need to look up the meaning?**

> **List the name of the town mentioned in the passage. Later, when you have more time, google that name. Some Biblical town names have a different name today. What do I know about that town? Have these places been mentioned in another passage of Scripture?**

> **What did I glean from this passage that I need to implement in my life? Take a minute to ask the Lord to help you implement these areas in your life.**

Step 3: PRAISE

All about Worship: Worship is merely praising the Lord for being God. Giving thanks and glory to the King of kings. On this page either write, sing, or find some way to show the God of all Creation gratitude for who He is to you. Thank Him for your breath, your life, providing everything you need, and for being a good good Father.

Worship Musical Group Albums recommended:

Lauren Daigle— Look up child

Mercy Me– Almost There

Bethel Music– You Make Me Brave, Victory (Live)

I am They– I am They

Passion– Follow you Anywhere

Hillsong Worship

Toby Mac– The Elements

Meredith Andrews– Worth it All

Chris McClarney—Breakthrough (Live)

Danny Gokey– Haven't Seen it Yet

Various Artists– Your Reckless Love

Rend Collective– The Art of Celebration

Mandisa– Overcomer, What If we were Real, Out of the Dark

Shane & Shane

Tauren Wells

Or google Christian Radio and choose your favorite station and listen to a song or two for the next five minutes. If you like to write your praise down, here is a space for you. If you sing a song, write the title of the song in the box to help you remember the joy you found today.

DAY 5: Step 1- PRAY

Date: _____

Good morning _____,

1.

2.

3.

4.

5.

6.

7.

Father, thank you for the people I'm blessed to love. Lord, I place

_____

_____

_____

_____ in your hands.

Father help me love my neighbors as You love them. Father, please help...

Free space to add any other requests...

Lord before I open Your Word, I ask you to open my eyes to see what YOU want to reveal to me today.

In the precious name of Jesus I pray all these things,

_____.

Step 2: READ

Scripture read today: _____

What does this passage show me about God's character?

God is faithful to His promises. What promise did you read about today?

What numbers did I see in the Scripture? Why was that detail mentioned?

What word or phrases stood out to me and why?

What word/s do I need to look up the meaning?

List the name of the town mentioned in the passage. Later, when you have more time, google that name. Some Biblical town names have a different name today. What do I know about that town? Have these places been mentioned in another passage of Scripture?

What did I glean from this passage that I need to implement in my life? Take a minute to ask the Lord to help you implement these areas in your life.

Step 3: PRAISE

All about Worship: Worship is merely praising the Lord for being God. Giving thanks and glory to the King of kings. On this page either write, sing, or find some way to show the God of all Creation gratitude for who He is to you. Thank Him for your breath, your life, providing everything you need, and for being a good good Father.

Worship Musical Group Albums recommended:

Lauren Daigle— Look up child

Mercy Me– Almost There

Bethel Music– You Make Me Brave, Victory (Live)

I am They– I am They

Passion– Follow you Anywhere

Hillsong Worship

Toby Mac– The Elements

Meredith Andrews– Worth it All

Chris McClarney—Breakthrough (Live)

Danny Gokey– Haven't Seen it Yet

Various Artists– Your Reckless Love

Rend Collective– The Art of Celebration

Mandisa– Overcomer, What If we were Real, Out of the Dark

Shane & Shane

Tauren Wells

Or google Christian Radio and choose your favorite station and listen to a song or two for the next five minutes. If you like to write your praise down, here is a space for you. If you sing a song, write the title of the song in the box to help you remember the joy you found today.

DAY 6: Step 1- PRAY

Date: _____

Good morning _____ ,

1.

2.

3.

4.

5.

6.

7.

Father, thank you for the people I'm blessed to love. Lord, I place

_____

_____

_____

_____in your hands.

Father help me love my neighbors as You love them. Father, please help...

Free space to add any other requests...

Lord before I open Your Word, I ask you to open my eyes to see what YOU want to reveal to me today.

In the precious name of Jesus I pray all these things,

_____.

Step 2: READ

Scripture read today: _____

What does this passage show me about God's character?

God is faithful to His promises. What promise did you read about today?

What numbers did I see in the Scripture? Why was that detail mentioned?

What word or phrases stood out to me and why?

What word/s do I need to look up the meaning?

List the name of the town mentioned in the passage. Later, when you have more time, google that name. Some Biblical town names have a different name today. What do I know about that town? Have these places been mentioned in another passage of Scripture?

What did I glean from this passage that I need to implement in my life? Take a minute to ask the Lord to help you implement these areas in your life.

Step 3: PRAISE

All about Worship: Worship is merely praising the Lord for being God. Giving thanks and glory to the King of kings. On this page either write, sing, or find some way to show the God of all Creation gratitude for who He is to you. Thank Him for your breath, your life, providing everything you need, and for being a good good Father.

Worship Musical Group Albums recommended:

Lauren Daigle— Look up child

Mercy Me– Almost There

Bethel Music– You Make Me Brave, Victory (Live)

I am They– I am They

Passion– Follow you Anywhere

Hillsong Worship

Toby Mac– The Elements

Meredith Andrews– Worth it All

Chris McClarney—Breakthrough (Live)

Danny Gokey– Haven't Seen it Yet

Various Artists– Your Reckless Love

Rend Collective– The Art of Celebration

Mandisa– Overcomer, What If we were Real, Out of the Dark

Shane & Shane

Tauren Wells

Or google Christian Radio and choose your favorite station and listen to a song or two for the next five minutes. If you like to write your praise down, here is a space for you. If you sing a song, write the title of the song in the box to help you remember the joy you found today.

Conclusion

My sweet friend, You did it! Being consistent every week isn't easy. But the rewards from completing this study are priceless. Ending a study can be bittersweet. We have grown accustom to our new routine and fellowship. But this study is unique, it doesn't have to end.

A 15 Minute "Date" with God can remain a part of your morning routine. This study helped lay the foundation God already provided for you. As you continue each morning, you will feel right at home with God. These *"dates"* with God are lasting, providing you with all that you need.

> For the Lord made this promise to David: *"And I will provide a place for my people Israel and will plant them so that they can have a home of their own and no longer be disturbed. Wicked people will not oppress them anymore, as they did at the beginning."*
>
> *-1 Chronicles 17:9 (NIV)*

These morning dates with God will open your eyes to see God's wonders. You will be able to hear Him lead you along the path He has marked out for you. With boldness stand firm in the promises of God. Everything God creates has a purpose, including the Bible.

> *"All Scripture is God-breathed and is useful for teaching, rebuking, correcting, and training in righteousness, so that the servant of God may be thoroughly equipped for every good work."*
>
> *-1 Timothy 3:16 (NIV)*

This passage informs us those 15 minute Dates with the Lord have a purpose as well. They're to equip you for the good work He has spoken over you. When God speaks over us, we need to pay close attention to His Words, for they will give you life.

Before I leave you, I want to share a Psalm David wrote out of a heart of gratitude for the goodness of the Lord and His provision.

> *"On the day I called, You answered me; You increased strength within me."*
>
> *-Psalm 138: 3(NIV)*

The theme in my Bible for this chapter of Psalm says, "God works out his plans for our lives and will bring us through the difficulties we face."

We endure the changing of seasons in our lives that mold us and shape us into the person we have become. Some of these seasons are harder than others. However, one thing remains constant during those seasons: God! God is ever-present, ever faithful, and always kind. We may not understand why the rug got pulled out from underneath us, but we know who will be there to pick us up and dust us off.

This verse reminds us of God's faithfulness. When we cry out to Him, he hears us. When we have a need, a genuine need, not a want, God always provides. Never forget where our blessing comes from, even during the good and bad seasons. Our seasons will ever be changing, and thank the Lord, they don't last forever. So, WORSHIP during your Worry.

Because, one thing will always remain the same… God is in control, God is good, and God is constant. Remembering this truth and seeking the Lord's blessing for each day builds our awareness of the Lord's movements. They may be small, but they are always there. David thanked God for the strength He blessed him with to endure the trials he was facing. We, too, can find something to be grateful for, even if it's the oxygen we breathe or the warm shower this morning.

God has greatness in store for you! Hold onto Him with each step you take. God knows the way and will guide your path. Sweet friend, you can trust His timing, His way, and His plan. All you need to do is just take His hand.

Thank you for allowing me to walk with you through these 40 days. It was an honor and a privilege for me to share with you. God has transformed my life with our Dates. If you would like to share with me about things you gleaned from this study, I would love to hear how God transformed you as well. You can find me several ways: (www.hooks2crook.com, Facebook Group: Hooks2Crook SOD, Instagram @hooks2crook, or Twitter @Hooks2C)

Final Evaluation

After you completed your dates with God, here is a little evaluation to help you evaluate your intimacy with God. You took this same evaluation at the beginning of the 6 weeks.

1. On a scale from 0 to 10, (0 being never and 10 being all the time): Where would you rate your relationship with God? How close are you with Him?

| 0 | 5 | 10 |

2. On a scale from 0 to 10, (0 being never and 10 being all the time): How often do you pray about offering Him glory, discussing choices, asking for His will to be done?

| 0 | 5 | 10 |

3. On a scale from 0 to 10, (0 being never and 10 being all the time): How often do you open up His Word throughout your week?

| 0 | 5 | 10 |

4. On a scale from 0 to 10, (0 being never and 10 being all the time): How often do you seek for answers in God's Word?

| 0 | 5 | 10 |

5. On a scale from 0 to 10, (0 being never and 10 being all the time): How often do you sing or offer praise to the Lord for being such a good God?

| 0 | 5 | 10 |

Leader's Guide

Prep before Week 1:   Leaders, thank you for taking this challenge. As you can see, this study is unique and might be out of your comfort zone. May I ease your mind? I will walk you through each week before you begin to read the Old and New Testaments Overviews on pages 200-203. You will utilize the back of this book the most. As you read those overviews, seek the Lord for His guidance on which two or three Books you should offer for your group to study during this time. Feel free to highlight two or three choices in the overview section to remember the Books He has pointed you towards. During the first gathering, your group will choose from the two or three books you suggest.

Week 1:   Welcome the ladies to your new Bible Study. Before you begin, play a little "icebreaker" to help your ladies get to know each other.

Ask the ladies to introduce themselves (first and last name) and then describe to the group their ideal "date."

Here is an example of what they can list.

- *Location*
- *Weather*
- *Time of day*
- *Who would you be with?*

After everyone has a turn to respond, open up in Prayer before you begin your review.

When beginning the study:

♦ Read the "Introduction" and "How Does it Work" with your ladies.

♦ Have the group take the First Evaluation to evaluate their personal relationship with God. (Allow this to be self-reflection, not a group discussion.)

♦ Run through the layout of the study with your ladies. *"Each week's activities are based on your personal time with God. There are three sections to complete each day. Each section is broken down into three 5-minute intervals. Do your best to complete the highlighted section for each week."*

After you have allowed time for the ladies to look through the sections for this week's homework, check to see if there are any questions. Then, offer two to three books of the Bible that were laid on your heart to read during this 6-week study. Once the group has chosen their Book of the Bible, Read Week One as a group and work through day one. Remind them only to complete the highlighted sections first. If time permits to work through the other sections, then continue working till the time is up. Set a timer for 5 minutes before starting each section.

Leader's Guide

⇒ After completing each section, ask your ladies, *"How was that? This can be practical to complete every morning. As the week goes on, you will become more comfortable with the structure, just like with any 'date' the first couple of times can feel a little awkward."*
⇒ Ease their minds and be gentle as you lead. This is new to some/most of them.

Thank each of the ladies for sharing today. Ask for any prayer requests. Close with prayer.

Week 2: Welcome the women to Session 2 of *A 15 Minute "Date" with God.* Open up with a word of Prayer.

Discuss the previous week:

- What did you enjoy about your date with God this week?
- Where did you struggle this week to complete the Homework?
- Offer helpful tips and encourage them to keep pressing on. Praise the ladies for their accomplishments and for completing their first week.

- What did you list as some of the Characteristics of God during your reading?
- Why is it essential for us to acknowledge these Characteristics of God?
- Were there any words you looked up that caught your attention?
- Was there a particular verse that stood out to you as you read this week?

- What was it about this verse that resonated with you?

Read the Beginning of Week 2 as a group.

Discuss what this week holds for them.

Thank each of the ladies for sharing today. Ask for any prayer requests. Close with prayer.

Week 3: Welcome the women to Session 3 of *A 15 Minute "Date" with God.* Open up with a word of Prayer.

Discuss the previous week:

- What did you enjoy about your date with God this week?

- Where did you struggle this week to complete the Homework?

- Offer helpful tips and encouragement to keep pressing on. Praise the ladies for their accomplishments for completing their second week.

- God is faithful to His promises. Have you discovered any promises of God during your reading?

Leader's Guide

- Would anyone like to share some of the songs they wrote down this week?

Read the Beginning of Week 3 as a group.

Discuss what this week holds for them. Remember, this week will be hard for your ladies if they dig deep. Addressing our sin isn't easy, but God requires it.

Thank each of the ladies for sharing today. Ask for any prayer requests. Close with prayer.

Week 4: Welcome the women to Session 4 of *A 15 Minute "Date" with God.* Open up with a word of Prayer.

Discuss the previous week:

- What did you enjoy about your date with God this week?

- Where did you struggle this week to complete the Homework?

- Offer helpful tips and encouragement to keep pressing on. Praise the ladies for their accomplishments for completing their second week.

- How did this week go? Confessing sins can be hard, yet freeing all at the same time. This process takes time and the enemy will try to remind you of these past areas of your life, but remember the freedom you found in Jesus. No one can take that away from you, not even Satan himself.

- Offer request for prayer here. Build a hedge of protection around your group by asking Jesus to protect their minds and hearts as they continue with this study.

- During your reading this week, were there any words that caught your attention that you chose to look up?

- Was there a particular verse that stood out to you as you read this week?

- What was it about this verse that resonated with you?

Leader's Guide

Read the Beginning of Week 4 as a group.

Discuss what this week holds for them. Remind the group of the importance of forgiving those who have wronged you. Holding a grudge places a wedge between in your relationships with God.

Thank each of the ladies for sharing today. Ask for any prayer requests. Close with prayer.

Week 5: Welcome the women to Session 5 of *A 15 Minute "Date" with God.* Open up with a word of Prayer.

Discuss the previous week:

- What did you enjoy about your date with God this week?

- Where did you struggle this week to complete the Homework?

- Offer helpful tips and encouragement to keep pressing on. Praise the ladies for their accomplishments for completing their fourth week.

- These past two weeks, as you have focused on forgiveness, have you been able to embrace freedom through forgiveness?

- Processing through the forgiveness of self and others takes time. If you're struggling with forgiveness, it's understandable. Remember, His grace is sufficient. It's not our grace we extend, but His grace. Forgiveness takes time because we are human. Keep pursuing the freedom found in forgiveness.

Read the Beginning of Week 5 as a group.

Discuss what this week holds for them.

Thank each of the ladies for sharing today. Ask for any prayer requests. Close with prayer.

Week 6: Welcome the women to Session 6 of *A 15 Minute "Date" with God*, your last week of study. Remind them you will meet one last time next week to review the Homework and take the Final Evaluation. Open with a word of Prayer.

Discuss the previous week:

- What did you enjoy about your date with God this week?

- Where did you struggle this week to complete the Homework?

- Offer helpful tips and encouragement to keep pressing on. Praise the ladies for their accomplishments for completing their fifth week.

Leader's Guide

- What did you list as some of the Characteristics of God during your reading?

- Was there a particular verse that stood out to you as you read this week? What was it about this verse that resonated with you?

Read the Beginning of Week 6 as a group.

Discuss what this week holds for them.

Thank each of the ladies for sharing today. Ask for any prayer requests. Close with prayer.

Week 7:   Welcome the women to Session 7 of *A 15 Minute "Date" with God,* your final
session. Open up with a word of Prayer.

Discuss the previous week:

- What did you enjoy about your date with God throughout these past 6 weeks?

- Are there areas your still struggling to uphold your "Date" with God?

- This week during your last session, you will complete the Final Evaluation ranking on page 190. Inform the group that you will talk a little bit about their findings during this session.

After they complete their Final Evaluation:

- Ask if they saw growth from their First Evaluation to the Final Evaluation.
- What kind of differences do they see?
- Are there still ways you would like to improve on? What are those areas, and how do you plan to achieve that goal?
- Is *A 15 Minute "Date" with God* something you will continue?
- Thank each of the ladies for sharing today. Ask for any prayer requests.

Close with prayer.

The Names of God: [2]

Elohim– God (Gen. 1:1) The strong Creator
Jehovah– LORD (Gen. 2:4) The self-existing One
Adonai– LORD/Master (Gen. 15:2) The Headship Name

The Compound Names of the LORD God:

"Jehovah El and Jehovah Elohim" Jehovah El Elohim (Josh. 22:22) the LORD God of Gods
Jehovah Elohim (Gen 2:4; 3:9-13, 21) The LORD God
Jehovah Elohe Abothekem (Josh 18:3) The LORD God of Your Fathers
Jehovah El Elyon (Gen 14:22) The LORD, the Highest God
Jehovah El Emeth (Ps 31:5) LORD God of Truth
Jehovah Elohim Tsebaoth (Ps 59:5, Isa 28:22) LORD God of Host
Jehovah El Gemuwal (Jer. 51: 56) The LORD God of Recompenses
Jehovah Elohe Yeshuathi (Ps 88:1) LORD God of My Salvation
Jehovah Elohe Yisrael (Ps 41:13) The LORD God of Israel

Compound Names of GOD

"El, Elohim and Elohe" Elohim (Gen 1:1) God
Elohim Bashamayim (Josh 2:11) God in Heaven
El Bethel (Gen 35:7) God of the House of GOD
Elohe Chaseddi (Ps 59:10) The God of My Mercy
Elohe Yisrael (Gen 33:20) God, the God of Israel
El Elyon (Gen 14:18; Ps 78:56, Dan 3:26) The Most High God
El Emunah (Deut 7:9) The Faithful God
El Gibbor (Isa 9:6) Mighty God
El Hakabodh (Ps 29:3) The God of Glory
El Hay (Josh 3:10; Jer 23:36; Dan 3:26) The Living God
El Hayyay (Ps 42:8) God of My Life
Elohim Kedoshim (Josh 24:19) Holy God
El Kanna (Exod 20:5) Jealous God
Elohe Mauzi (Ps 43:2) God of My Strength
Elohim Machase Lanu (Ps 62:8) God Our Refuge
Eli Maelekhi (Ps 68:24) God My King
El Marom (Mic 6:6) God Most High
El Nekamoth (Ps 18: 47) God that Avengeth
El Nose (Ps 99:8) God that Forgave
Elohim Ozer Li (Ps 54:4) God My Helper
El Rai (Gen 16:13) God Seest Me
Elsali (Ps 42:9) God, My Rock
El Shaddai (Gen 17:1, 2, Ezek 10:5) Almighty God

The Names of God: [2]

El Simchath Gili (Ps 43:4) God My Exceeding Joy
Elohim Shophtim Ba-arets (Ps 58:11) God that Judgeth in the Earth
Elohim Tsebaoth (Ps 80:7, Jer 35:17, 38:17) God of Hosts
Elohe Tishuathi (Ps 18:46; 51:14) God of My Salvation
Elohe Tsadeki (Ps 4:1) God of My Righteousness
Elohe Yakob (Ps 20:1) God of Israel

The Compound Name of Jehovah

Jehovah (Exod 6:2, 3) The LORD
Adonia Jehovah (Gen 15:2) Lord God
Jehovah Adon Kol Ha-arets (Josh 3:11) The LORD, the Lord of All the Earth
Jehovah Bore (Isa 40:28) The LORD Creator
Jehovah Elyon (Gen 14:18-20) The LORD Most High
Jehovah Chereb (Deut 33:29) The Lord...the Sword
Jehovah Eli (Ps 18:2) The LORD My God
Jehovah Maginnenu (Ps 89:18) The LORD Our Defense
Jehovah Goelekh (Isa 49:26; 60:16) The LORD Thy Redeemer
Jehovah Hashopet (Judg 11:27) The LORD the Judge
Jehovah Hoshiah (Ps 20:9) O LORD Save
Jehovah Immeka (Judg 6:12) The LORD is with You
Jehovah Izuz Wegibbor (Ps 24:8) The LORD Strong and Mighty
Jehovah Kabodhi (Ps 3:3) The LORD My God
Jehovah Kanna Shemo (Exod 34:14) The LORD Whose Name is Jealous
Jehovah Tsuri (Ps 19:14) O LORD My Strength
Jehovah Keren-Yishi (Ps 18:2) The LORD the Horn of My Salvation
Jehovah Machsi (Ps 91:9) The LORD My Refuge
Jehovah Magen (Deut 33:29) The LORD the Shield
Jehovah Makkeh (Ezek 7:9) The LORD that Smiteth
Jehovah Mauzzam (Ps 37:39) The LORD Their Strength
Jehovah Mauzzi (Jer 16:19) The LORD My Fortress
Ha-Melech Jehovah (Ps 98:6) The LORD the King
Jehovah Melech Olam (Ps 10:16) The LORD King Forever
Jehovah Mephalti (Ps 18:2) The LORD My Deliverer
Jehovah Mekaddishkem (Exod 31:13) The LORD that Sanctifies You
Jehovah Moshiekh (Isa 49:26; 60:16) The LORD Your Savior

The Names of God: [2]

Jehovah Nissi (Exod 17:15) The LORD My Banner
Jehovah Ori (Ps 27:1) The LORD My Light
Jehovah Uzzi (Ps 28:7) The LORD My Strength
Jehovah Rophe (Exod 15:26) The LORD (our) Healer
Jehovah Sabaoth (Tsebaoth) (1Sam 1:3) The LORD of Hosts
Jehovah Sali (Ps 18:2) The LORD My Rock
Jehovah Shalom (Judg 6:24) The LORD (our) Peace
Jehovah Shammah (Ezek 48:35) The LORD Is There

Old Testament Book Summary

Genesis: The first book of the Bible. Genesis takes you through the creation of the World, the fall of man, and the need for restoration. It reveals the story of Abraham and the fulfillment of God's promises.

Exodus: The story of how God used Moses to free His people from Egypt.

Leviticus: A handbook of procedures for the Levites (priest). This book discussions the roles and duties for priest in worship. Leviticus reveals the way to live holy and set apart.

Numbers: The story of the Israel's first attempt to enter the Promised Land and how fear prevents them from believing in God's promises and entering the land. Israel endured consequences for their disobedience. After 40 years of wandering, Israel trusted God's word and made plans to enter their promised land.

Deuteronomy: The word Deuteronomy means "Second Law." As the Israelites wandered, God spoke through Moses, laying out His commands. God gives the people a glimpse of the promise, but they refused to believe God's provisions. Israel reacted to their fears and chose to be disobedient. Their consequence was to wander in the wilderness longer.

Joshua: Joshua becomes the new leader for Israel after Moses passes away. He leads the people of God to claim their Promised Land. There are many victorious battles and divisions of land recorded in this book.

Judges: There is a recurring cycle present: Israel sins; their enemies place heavy burdens on them. The people of Israel confess sin and ask God for deliverance. God raises judges who reveal the sins of Israel and call them to repent.

Ruth: A Story of a daughter-in-law caring for her mother-in-law. A love story of a kinsmen redeemer showing love to his new bride.

1 Samuel: Records the life of Samuel, the last judge, who anointed Saul to be the first king of Israel and then anoints David to be king once God's favor left Saul.

2 Samuel: Historical record of David's rule showing how a good leader rules by placing God on the throne of their heart.

1 Kings: Israel is divided into two kingdoms: North and South (Israel and Judah). The Northern Kingdom had no good kings, while The Southern Kingdom had two good kings (Hezekiah & Josiah). You will learn how bad kings and their horrible choices having rippling effects on their people.

2 Kings: This book warns rulers what their fate will look like if they choose not to serve God alone.

Old Testament Book Summary:

1 Chronicles: This book was written to unify God's people. It traces the linage of David's bloodline and teaches us how to worship.

2 Chronicles: Israel bonds through their worship of God. The kings of Judah are compared by their religious rulers and the evil rulers.

Ezra: God is faithful to His promises by restoring His people to their promised land after the Babylonian Exile.

Nehemiah: This book is about being faithful to God and rebuilding a wall that would protect the people of God. We read about the process Nehemiah took to build the wall and how he joined the people together to get it done.

Esther: We read about the bravery of a young woman as she stands up for God's people before the king who was about to murder them all because of foolish and bitter counsel.

Job: This book describes the life of a man who suffered many disasters, yet he remains faithful to God.

Psalms: This is a large book. You can find it in the middle of the Bible. Many people wrote the book of Psalms, but King David wrote most of the book. David was known for being a man after God's own heart. Psalms is a book that holds many of David's intimate prayers to the Father-showing you how personal God desires to be with all of us.

Proverbs: King Solomon wrote Proverbs. He was known to be the wisest king of all Israel. Proverbs is a book of wisdom. Wisdom literature provides absolute truths but not absolute guarantees.

Ecclesiastics: King Solomon wrote this book warning us that if we live a life apart from God, it will all be meaningless.

Song of Songs: This is a very detailed love story between a bride and her bridegroom that could make you blush.

Isaiah: The Prophet warns his people not to serve any god but the One True God.

Jeremiah: He inquires the Israel nation to turn away from their sins of worshiping other gods and back to the One True Living God.

Lamentations: A book that speaks of how disobedience welcomes disaster. You also will read how in our suffering, God suffers with us.

Ezekiel: He announces God's judgment on Israel and other nations. This book also shares the salvation promise God will fulfill in the future.

Old Testament Book Summary:

Daniel: Daniel is a book about a man who remained faithful to God in the midst of kings who opposed God. Daniel shows us how to abide by the authority of man, but understand God's rule is the first rule we submit to even if our leaders resists God's authority. It foretells of the end of times and of Jesus.

Hosea: A story of a prophet who was told to love a prostitute to give the people of Israel an image of the way God loves them.

Joel: He warns Israel of God's judgment for sin and beckons the people to turn back to God.

Amos: This book is about God's judgment on the Northern Kingdom who turned to complacency, idolatry, and refused to help the poor.

Obadiah: God judges those people who have harmed Israel.

Jonah: God sends a prophet to warn the nation about God's judgment. But after they hear the message of God, they turn from their ways seeking God's forgiveness and grace. God shows them mercy.

Micah: This book warns Israel again about the coming judgment and how if they repent, God will pardon them.

Nahum: He proclaimed the judgment of Assyria and offers comfort to Judah with God's truth.

Habakkuk: God is still in control despite what the world looks like or the circumstances.

Zephaniah: Makes Judah aware of their complacency and point them to return to God.

Haggai: This book is about God's people rebuilding the His temple.

Zechariah: He reveals the future deliverance of God's people through the Messiah.

Malachi: He confronts the people of their sin and to restore their relationship with the LORD.

New Testament Book Summary

Matthew: This book was written for a Jewish audience. The view of this record was from a disciple of Jesus named Matthew, who was a tax collector. Matthew documents the lineage of Jesus and the story of his life.

Mark: This book, written by Mark, who studied under Peter records the life of Jesus at the start of His ministry through Peter's eyes.

Luke: Luke wrote this book as a historical and physical record about the life of Jesus, from birth to death and resurrection. Luke is considered the most detailed gospel account.

John: This is the fourth historical record of the life of Jesus and is written by John, who was one of the first disciples follow Jesus.

Acts: This book, written after the resurrection of Jesus, is the record of the start and spread of the Christian Church. It was through their persecution from Saul (who later becomes Paul) the life, death, and resurrection of Jesus became known worldwide. The name of Jesus was proclaimed birthing the religious faith of Christianity.

Romans: This is a letter from Paul to the Roman Christians offering them instruction and a glimpse of his message. Romans is known for the "Roman Road to Salvation," underlining the meaning behind what it means to surrender to Jesus as your Lord and Savior.

1 Corinthians: A letter from Paul to the Church of Corinth describes things they were doing wrong and offers them solutions to strengthen the body of believers.

2 Corinthians: This letter from Paul to the Church of Corinth is written to help them identify false teachers.

Galatians: Paul wrote this letter to churches in southern Galatia. Paul was correcting the Jewish people who were placing their customs and rituals onto the Gentiles who believed Jesus was their Savior. Paul educated the Judiazers, the Jewish people, that it is through Jesus freedom is found. Paul explains the importance of not placing unnecessary "rules" on their fellow Gentiles to ensure their faith development.

Ephesians: Paul wrote to the church in Ephesus, encouraging them to unite as the body of Christ. Paul describes the nature and purpose of the Body of Believers.

New Testament Book Summary:

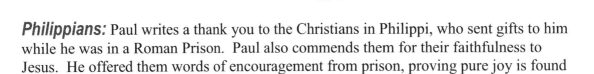

Philippians: Paul writes a thank you to the Christians in Philippi, who sent gifts to him while he was in a Roman Prison. Paul also commends them for their faithfulness to Jesus. He offered them words of encouragement from prison, proving pure joy is found in Jesus Christ alone.

Colossians: Paul writes this letter to the church in Colossae, who added false expectations and philosophies to the Christian doctrine. Paul is straightforward, identifying Jesus is the ONLY Way and all you need.

1 Thessalonians: A letter to the church of Thessalonica from Paul, assuring them Jesus will return. This message guides believers to true faith. Paul helps remove the confusion they had on when Jesus would return.

2 Thessalonians: Paul writes this letter a few months after the first to clear up the remaining confusion they still had about the second coming of Jesus.

1 Timothy: Timothy was a young leader that served under Paul. This letter to Timothy was from Paul. The letter encouraged Timothy to remain faithful to God with clear instructions on how to lead and serve God's people.

2 Timothy: Paul is in jail again and decides to write to Timothy. The significance of this letter is Paul passes the baton for his ministry to Timothy. The letter is the final instruction Paul will give to Timothy, who is the pastor of the church in Ephesus.

Titus: Paul writes this letter to advise Titus as he monitored and oversaw all the churches on the island of Crete. Paul knew Titus needed guidance after sending him to the island. This letter provides Titus with his job description and how to accomplish his job.

Philemon: Philemon had a slave that ran away. Paul writes to Philemon asking him to forgive his slave, Onesimus, and accept him as Philemon's brother in Christ.

Hebrews: Many strong men of the faith wrote Hebrews to reassure the Jewish Christians that Jesus was the Messiah. This letter reminds us of the superiority of Jesus and our need for Him.

James: The brother of Jesus is the author of this book. Jesus appeared to James after the resurrection, confirming He was the Messiah. James becomes the leader of the Jerusalem church. James writes to expose and inform on the misleading practices Christians might find themselves doing. However, James helps us refocus on the truth and how to live like Christ.

1 Peter: Christians where being persecuted during the time of this letter. Peter offers words of encouragement, hoping to strengthen the faith of the Jewish Christians who were forced from their home.

New Testament Book Summary:

2 Peter: Peter writes to the church as a whole. In this letter, he points out false teachings to recognize and encourages them to mature in their faith. Building their confidence in their growing knowledge of Jesus Christ.

1 John: The apostle John wrote this letter to the new generations of believers. He shared with them encouraging words and ways to expose and counter false teachings.

2 John: The apostle John wrote this letter some believe to a woman and her family. The reason for this letter was to identify the basics of following Jesus: truth and love. He also warned against false teachings in this letter.

3 John: This letter written by the apostle John was thanking Gaius for his hospitality he offered to church leaders who travel.

Jude: Jude is another brother of Jesus and James wrote to the Jewish Christians. Jude reminded the Jewish Christians about the need to stand firm in the truth of Christ and watch out for false teachings.

Revelation: John writes the final book of the Bible. This book reveals markers for the second coming of Jesus. This book identifies the fullness of Christ and offers warnings and hope to believers.

Resource Page

Commentaries: Matthew Henry's Commentary in Volume One
The Tony Evans Bible Commentary

Reference Books: Pictorial Bible Dictionary with Topical Index
Vine's Complete Expository Dictionary of Old and New Testament
Words the Lyman's Bible Encyclopedia

Websites: https://www.preceptaustin.org/
https://www.biblegateway.com/
https://www.logos.com/
http://www.jewishwikipedia.info/jewish_calendar.html
https://bible.org/question/what-significance-numbers-scripture
https://www.blueletterbible.org/

EndNotes

1. Foster, Jeremy. "First Things First." 5 January 2020, Hope City, Houston, TX, Sermon.
2. Evans, Tony. Tony Evans Bible Commentary. Holman Bible Publishers, Nashville, Tennessee.2019.
3. Shirer, Priscilla. "FAQ." Going Beyond Ministries, goingbeyond.com/ministry/ministry-faqs. Accessed 3 March. 2020.
4. TerKeurst, Lysa. "Establishing a Biblical Framework for Writers/Teaching/ Speaking." She Speaks. 6 Sept. 2019, Carterville, Il.
5. Lauren Daigle. Lyrics to "First." Genius, 2020. genius.com/Lauren-daigle-first-lyrics.
6. Meredith Andrews. Lyrics to "Spirit of the Living God." Genius, 2020. genius.com/Meredith-andrews-spirit-of-the-living-god-lyrics
7. Bethel Music. Lyrics to "Reckless Love." Genius,2020. genius.com/Bethel-music-reckless-love-spontaneous-live-lyrics.
8. Tasha Cobb Leonard. Lyrics to "Break Every Chain." Genius, 2020. genius.com/Tasha-cobbs-leonard-break-every-chain-live-lyrics.
9. Elevation Worship. Lyrics to "Give Me Faith." Genius, 2020. genius.com/Elevation-worship-give-me-faith-lyrics.
10. Chris McClarney. Lyrics to "I'm Listening." Genius, 2020. genius.com/Chris-mcclarney-im-listening-lyrics.
11. Brooks, Peggy. Personal Interview. 27 February 2020.

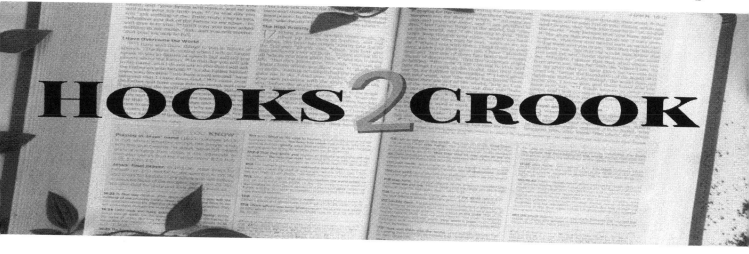

HOOKS2CROOK

Hooks2Crook encourages, equips, and endorses women to walk boldly in obedience to God. We use our God given gifts and talents to serve Him. We are women of valor, grace, and beauty through Christ Jesus, who equips us for His excellent work.

Encourage   -   Equip   -   Endorse

We are here to partner with you on your journey to your Promised Land.

Visit our site for more information:

www.hooks2crook.com

HOOKS2CROOK

Made in the USA
Monee, IL
30 May 2020